REMEMBRANCE

Front cover: Geoffrey and the three Tommies (Jersey War Tunnels)

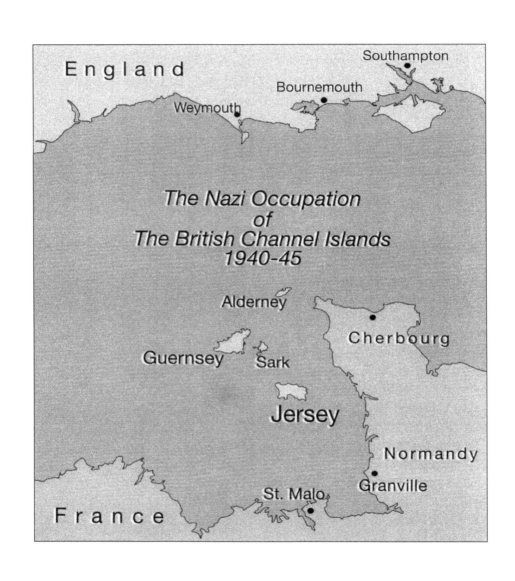

REMEMBRANCE

*Growing up under the Nazi Occupation
of the British Channel Islands, 1940–45*

J. G. MESSERVY NORMAN

Seeker
Publishing & Distribution
in the Channel Islands

Published in 2015 by
SEEKER PUBLISHING & DISTRIBUTION
Units 1 & 2 Elms Farm
La Route de la Hougue Mauger
St Mary
Jersey   JE3 3BA

www.seekerpublishing.com

Origination by
SEAFLOWER BOOKS
www.ex-librisbooks.co.uk

Printed by CPI Anthony Rowe
Chippenham, Wiltshire

ISBN 978-0-9932657-0-9

*In memory of
those who were there,
those who enriched our lives
and
those whom we fondly remember*

Contents

List of illustrations

Foreword

Some years ago I had occasion to visit the British Isle of Jersey, a wonderfully scenic Island, notably situated just off the coast of France. And there I heard a story I could hardly imagine, though it was a true story. Every word true.

At that time I was a writer/producer of American TV fare (*Dallas, MacGyver,* and the like) and felt privileged to have been invited by the States of Jersey to explore the possibilities of bringing American film production to the Island, and producing a TV series there.

I toured the Island locations with my partner and fellow writer Geoffrey Norman, seeing the ancient churches and castles, the picturesque bays, granite farmhouses and – to my astonishment – bunkers, bunkers, bunkers! German bunkers and battlements were everywhere, remnants of the German Occupation of the Island during World War II.

I was only vaguely aware of that bit of history but Geoffrey, Jersey born and bred, had actually lived it! Grew up under the Nazi Occupation – for five long years!

Geoffrey was three and a half when the Germans took the Island, and almost nine when the war ended and Jersey was liberated. To a child the world into which he's born is the world that is. Geoffrey's "normal" was to see the brutality that came with the war while going about the business of growing up – playing in the woods with the other little boys, trading the military junk and live ammunition which was everywhere on the Island, and sorting out the truly important things in life, like why little girls didn't have willies like little boys.

In his world it was normal that bikes had no tyres, that shoes were carved out of wood and soled with tin, and that by the end of the war everyone was starving to death.

I was enthralled as I listened to Geoffrey's stories of that time. He told them matter-of-factly, without intending to, because for him the incidents were simply the way it was. To me those stories were more remarkable than any I could make up, and I urged him to set them down.

Many histories are written, but few like this one, from someone who was there. The vignettes Geoffrey describes do more than recall a chronicle of that time; they speak to the character of a people, of the inner strength and values that sustained them through their ordeal.

I believe you will find *Remembrance* as moving and enjoyable as I did.

Calvin Clements Jr.

1   Red stripe and a peppermint

My earliest recollection of the German Occupation is that of a narrow red stripe running down the side of a pair of grey-green cavalry breeches – and a peppermint. I remember gazing wide-eyed as the man in red-striped breeches jovially knelt down beside me and prised two large round white peppermints out of a red and green wrapper.

"Here," said the officer with a light chuckle, after popping one of the mints into his mouth and offering me the other.

"*Ein für mir und* … one for you … *es ist gut, ja?*"

The seductive flavour of the chalky white mint exploded in my mouth! A taste I had never experienced before and certainly one that I was not about to forget.

It had been a little less than four months since Hitler's *Wehrmacht* Forces had landed and occupied the British Channel Islands on 1 July, 1940. The Germans had taken over the art deco sports stadium and indoor roller-skating rink located behind our house for use as a military supply storehouse, which the high-ranking staff officer with the roll of peppermints had come to inspect.

With the peppermint sweetly dissolving in my mouth, I turned from where I stood with the officer outside the stadium and excitedly cried out to my father as he emerged with his bicycle and closed the gate to our back garden.

"Daddy!" I cried. "Daddy!"

My father looked up and immediately, for some reason, I could tell from the look on his face that he was not too happy …

"Oh dear!" I thought, and quickly turned back to the tall soldier with the narrow red stripe running down the side of his trousers.

"May I have one for my daddy too?"

"One for your daddy?" asked the officer.

"Yes. One for my daddy," I replied. "Over there."

The officer looked up, and as his gaze met with that of my father's, the jovial twinkle in his eyes suddenly clouded into a cold, distant stare.

"No," he said without looking at me. "You go to your father now – *ja!*"

For the next five years, I would see that officer and many others like him strut the streets and byways of our Island, but I would never taste another peppermint.

~   ~   ~

Most people today are unaware that Hitler's German forces did in fact occupy and hold British soil during World War II.

In early 1940, after blitzkrieging[1] their way through France, the Germans kept going off the French coast and took the Islands of Jersey, Guernsey, Alderney, and Sark. Hitler immediately seized upon the propaganda value of having taken British soil and ordered the Islands to be defended and turned into total siege fortresses with eleven heavy batteries and thirty-eight strongpoints – more than the entire French coast from Dieppe to St Nazaire.

The British response to Hitler's Occupation, calculated upon the bloody cost of retaking the Islands being too high, was to leave those of us who remained, together with those who had been unable to evacuate to the British mainland, to fend for ourselves. Which is what we did – for five long years!

During that time, roughly 66,000 Islanders had to live cheek by jowl in an uneasy truce alongside roughly 45,000 occupying Nazi and German forces, including some 6,000 forced slave labourers.

Members of the Islands' small Jewish community were required to register and then denied the right to work. While some of them complied with the order, most were able to simply melt away into the general population.

Over the course of the Occupation, the Germans locally arrested and imprisoned some 4,000 people for breaking German Occupation law. Others who were less fortunate ended up in European concentration camps, some never to return. Therefore, left with no option other than to persevere and survive, we would have to bear up under what would become the most desperate of conditions.

Once the German Forces had occupied and taken over our Island, everything suddenly became scarce if not impossible to get hold of – the value of even the most insignificant article would change.

All necessary supplies, both civilian and military, had to be brought in via ship from occupied France, and a special purchasing commission for the basic requirements required by the civilian population (about 45,000 in Jersey) was installed in order to accomplish this. Naturally, rationing became the reality of the day.

The States of Jersey, the elected governing assembly of the Bailiwick of Jersey,

---

1 *The rapid mechanized armoured advance of the German forces.*

Nazi Germany arrives – 1940

The Bailiff, Alexander Coutanche, (second from left) and Attorney General Duret Aubin meet the Germans at the airport

1940–45
German military bands play in St Helier

created and set up a special civilian Superior Council comprising senior jurists and politicians in order to administer the Island's civil affairs in conjunction with Dr Casper, the Chief Administrator of the *Feldkommandantur* 515. My grandfather, James Messervy-Norman, a former diplomat, a Jurat[2] of the Royal Court, and a sitting member of the States of Jersey, the Island's government, was asked to serve on this special council by taking charge of communications,

---

2 *Jurats are judges of fact rather than law, and serve along with the Bailiff, who acts as presiding judge, to form the Royal (high) Court in the Bailiwicks of Jersey and Guernsey.*

transport, and public works.

I loved my grandfather; he knew everything! He had been the British, Norwegian, and Swedish Consul in Egypt and Custodian of Turkish Affairs after the First World War, and he had camped and shared a tent with General Allenby while on a pilgrimage together at Mount Sinai. He kept an armoury of swords, shields, and spears out of Livingstone's Africa in the main hallway of his home at Anneville Lodge. His armoury also included two tenth-century Abyssinian battleaxes inlaid with solid gold and silver. Grandpa, or rather Grumpa, as I had grown to know him, collected butterflies from all over the world and had a massive stamp collection, which included a full set of first issued penny blacks and blues. Best of all, he had answers for all my questions, and I would have many in the years to come.

Despite the ever-growing shortages of basic necessities, along with the crushing restrictions upon our liberty, the native adult population had no choice other than to soldier on in the face of mounting adversity. Defiantly, our parents held on to their traditional cultural values in order to retain a semblance of normality – if not for themselves, for us, their children. Those British values of pride and self-reliance would get us through the ordeal.

It would be a long time before the Allies did finally turn their attention to freeing us. It was not to be by an assault or invasion, but by pursuing a punishing blockade upon the Islands in order to strangle and starve the Germans into a full surrender. Needless to say, this meant we would starve too. Little did we know during the early years of the Occupation what we were in for, and what it would eventually require in order to survive.

~   ~   ~

2 Mandalay and the last summer

At the beginning of the Occupation, I lived with my parents in a semi-detached corner house named Altona, in the parish of St Clement, not too far from the granite slipway that ran down to the beach at Millard's Corner, and just across the road from the Jersey Canning Company, where my father worked as the managing director.

In order to avoid its confiscation by the Germans, my father had hidden away his beloved Morris Cowley coupe with special wire wheels under a tarpaulin, behind a wall of crated cans in the factory's main warehouse. This meant that each morning, in place of the car, I would ride to school on the homemade crossbar seat that my father haad installed on his bicycle.

Except for when it was raining, I found that I quite enjoyed our morning bike rides together, because then I could ask him a mountain of questions as we rode along the way to school, whereas in the car we usually arrived at the gate before I could ever think of anything really important to ask him.

Mandalay was a delightful little two-roomed schoolhouse that sat in a garden filled with fruit trees and flowers on the west side of a lovely old Edwardian house. The school and grounds were surrounded and well-concealed on three sides behind high granite walls, and it was there that I met most of the childhood friends who would accompany me on to Victoria College Prep School and then eventually on to the College itself.

Nigel Meeks, who lived in a house across the road and attended Mandalay with me, was my first and closest friend, and then in our immediate circle at Mandalay came Graeme (Titch) Cavey, Robert (Bob) Sowden, and Michael Drelaud, whom we all simply knew as just plain Drelaud. Being in class was not a favourite pastime for any of us, not when compared to mucking about outside in the gardens.

Miss Le Quesne taught the younger kids in one room, which would include my friends and me, while Miss Garnier taught the older kids in the other room. Both teachers were somewhat stern in their approach and I cannot recall ever having seen either one of these women so much as smile. But then, as they would say in those days: "There's a war on, remember!"

My father as I like to remember him.
1940, Anneville Lodge

Leaving for school
with my father, 1940

My mother, taking tea on
the beach. Summer 1940

My grandfather, Jurat James
Messervy-Norman, 1939

On a good day, Miss Le Quesne would issue each of us a large lump of Plasticine, out of which she instructed us to form and model letters of the alphabet, a task most of the kids in class were quite happy to get on with and do. Robert Sowden would start out with a concerted effort and usually manage to get as far as forming a skinny twisted-looking letter "A", before giving up to join our group effort in modelling a desktop full of soldiers, bombs, guns, tanks, helmets, and cannons – after all, there was a war on, remember! When Miss

Le Quesne saw our patriotic efforts she would explode into a diatribe about why it was that we couldn't behave like all the other children and concentrate on forming our ABCs. But then, what was so wrong with modelling an attack for an "A"; bombs for a "B"; cannons for a "C"; guns for a "G", and some soldiers and shells for an "S"?

Mandalay school play,
Christmas 1940
Geoffrey third from left, front row
Nigel circled, second from left

When school broke up for the summer holidays, and with German soldiers walking about everywhere, Nigel and I would spend most of our days playing on the huge sandy beach below the slipway at Millard's Corner, which was just a stone's throw away from the main gates to what I had come to know as "Daddy's factory".

Both Nigel's mother and mine would rent a couple of deckchairs from the attendant who, together with his wife, ran the beach concession out of a faded wooden tea kiosk near the top of the slipway. Our mothers would set themselves up on the warm, soft sand below the sea wall where they could keep an eye on us and chat about the war and why all the blasted, off-duty Germans were sunbathing and lounging about on the beach like a bunch of holidaymakers.

Nigel and I would run off to play in the tide pools until lemonade or ice cream time. After much begging and whining, we would run up to the kiosk armed with a silver sixpence and decide between a Smith's ice-cream cone and a fizzy lemonade, while our mothers followed along and bought a pot of tea for two on a tray, which they carried back to their deckchairs under the sea wall.

Towards the end of that summer, and much to our disappointment, the kiosk suddenly closed down. Having run out of tea, ice-cream cones and other wares, the owners had no choice other than to board up its service window and abandon the kiosk to further fade in the seasonal sun – a harbinger of what was to come.

By the middle of the following summer, the Germans had closed all the beaches, and a huge concrete bunker with its heavy gun commanding a lethal sweep across the bay now blocked the entire slipway leading down to our lovely beach.

Geoffrey, spring 1941

3   Rule Britannia on one

By the following summer holidays, my mother had given birth to my sister Diana. She was born on 7 June during a time when the Island now saw itself on a total war footing.

The Nazi *Organisation Todt*, known as the OT, a Third Reich civil and military engineering group named after its founder, Fritz Todt, had brought thousands of forced slave workers into the Channel Islands in order to fortify them against an Allied invasion.

Although these slave workers were deliberately ill-nourished and very badly treated, they also added to the overall strain and demand upon the Islands' limited resources. Most of them were still dressed in the tattered remains of what was left of the street clothing they were wearing on the day when they were picked up and pressed into forced labour from all across Europe. The Germans

Defiant "V" for victory sign, 1941

strictly forbade Islanders from feeding or helping any of these poor wretched souls, but that did not deter some of the Islanders from doing whatever they could when an opportunity presented itself. Roughly painted "V" for victory signs began to appear on walls and road signs much to the annoyance of the Abwehr/Gestapo, who in turn countered by offering a reward to anyone who would provide them with information leading to the persons responsible for insulting the face of German authority.

Everything immediately became increasingly scarce and even bread became rationed. Arrangements were made for communal meals for children, and Oberst Rudolf Graf von Schmettow was appointed military commander of the Channel Islands, with everyone being ordered to drive and ride on the right-hand side of the road. Of course this upset some of our local drivers, but most of the cars in private ownership on the Island had been requisitioned, if not confiscated and shipped off to France for use in the German war effort. For those who still had the use of a vehicle, any opposition to driving on the right-hand side of the road would have been pointless and futile under Occupation. As for my friends, and me, by the time we were able to ride our bikes to school, right-hand traffic was all that we had ever known.

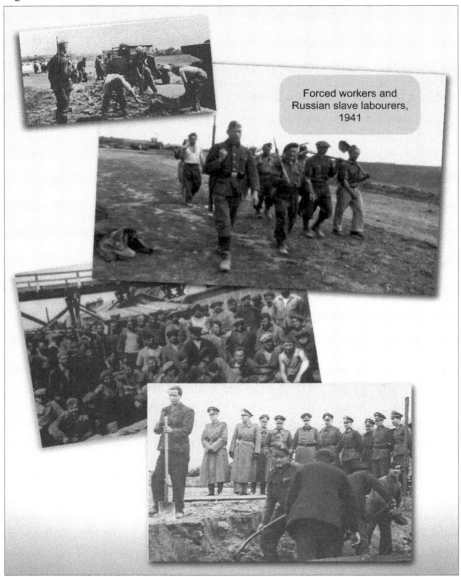

Forced workers and Russian slave labourers, 1941

Instead of going to the old beach up the road, everyone now went to the swimming pool on the beach down at Havre des Pas. This large catchment pool would refresh itself twice a day, at high tide. It had diving boards with lots of sunbathing terraces and changing cabins. Here I would meet up and play with Titch, Robert, and Drelaud, my classmates from Mandalay. On sunny days, one would hardly know that there was a war going on. Everyone, including the German soldiers, especially those billeted in the various surrounding hotels, loved "the pool". And I was often struck by the fact that I could see a happy, normal-looking fellow in red swimming trunks dive into the pool and then, a short time later, be completely taken aback upon seeing the same person emerge from the changing area in full German army uniform!

On Saturday mornings I would tag along behind my father as he walked up the road and crossed over onto the nine-hole golf course and head for the clubhouse where he and Paul Boleat, the assistant manager at "Daddy's factory", would pair up with another couple. New golf balls were no longer available and those who still owned and held one or two treated them like gold. Even the ones that had an ugly slice on one side due to a bad chip out of the rough could, like a candle or a pair of knitted socks, fetch a premium price. So most of the time, while my father and his friends played the greens, my mates and I would search along the banks of the shallow brook that divided the course to see if we could find any lost balls.

On one particular Saturday, as I followed my father and his friends off the first tee, there came a massive boom followed by a whining screech overhead. The Germans had set up several large field guns on the far north side of Pallot's marsh, from where they were test-firing some heavy field guns aimed high overhead and out to sea. Each time they fired, I would look up and sometimes actually see the red-hot shell as it screamed on its way over and beyond my friend Elizabeth Colley's house. On the other hand, my father and his friends refused to even acknowledge the German activity, let alone look up, preferring instead to continue with their game as though it

Coastal bunker

was just another quiet Saturday morning on the golf course. My father chipped with an eight iron and landed on the far corner of the green leaving him, unlike the others, with a long putt to the hole. While the sporadic booming blasts from the guns sent their screaming shells through the morning sky, the other players managed to sink their balls after a couple of putts for a par. Then it was my father's turn to address his long and somewhat difficult putt with hardly any expectation for a birdie under the screaming intermittent overhead conditions. But knowing how much my father hated the Germans and their Occupation, I could immediately sense his intense stubborn determination as he lined the ball up, not to let the "damned Jerries" and their guns get in the way of his Saturday morning game. Ignoring the guns and the overhead scream, I held my breath and watched as the ball rolled and meandered its way towards the edge of the hole, where it curled around the rim and dropped for a birdie!

Rule Britannia!

~   ~   ~

4 The move to La Blinérie

My recollections of 1942 still lie half-submerged somewhere beneath the chilling darkness of a grey wartime sky. By the second year of the Occupation, everything seemed to have taken on the tired grey-green pallor of the Nazi war machine.

As kids, we sought and collected pre-war pictures and cigarette cards depicting anything wearing a British uniform. Life for us as children continued in our normal routine from day to day, others were not so fortunate. On the dark, grey morning of 17 March, 1941, the Germans tied a twenty-year-old Frenchman named François Scornet to a tree in the leafy grounds of St Ouen's Manor and executed him by firing squad. Scornet and a couple of his compatriots had tried to escape from France to England in a small open boat. Unfortunately, the lads mistook Guernsey for the English coast, resulting in their capture.

I remember overhearing my mother telling someone how the Germans, while on their way to the execution, had pulled up in their lorry outside a bar on the esplanade, leaving Scornet to sit on his coffin in the back of the lorry under guard while they had a beer before continuing on to fulfill their grizzly detail.

The execution of Scornet shattered many illusions. Islanders had become complacent by the everyday interaction with the Germans – on our streets, in the shops, on the beaches, etc. – we were jolted back to the reality that we were living under the gun. No more would it be business as usual.

Around the end of May, Colonel Knackfuss, *Feldkommandant* of the German *Feldkommandantur* 515, informed the Bailiff[3] and Superior Council that all wireless sets were to be confiscated on the basis of Article 53 of the Hague Convention.

François Scornet 1914-41
Executed by firing squad in the gardens of
St Ouen's manor, 17 March, 1941

---

3 *The Office of the Bailiff (the chief commoner) of Jersey – from Anglo-Norman French 'guardian of the pleas of the Crown'.*

Naturally, this upset everyone. Fortunately, my father was able to get Angus MacBeth, his chief engineer at the factory, to get hold of a crystal set and a pair of earphones for him. Mr Mac, as I knew him, was a big, burly Scott who had come to Jersey from the Isle of Skye. He and his wife lived in one of the factory cottages with their little black-and-white terrier. Mr Mac ran the factory canteen and my father was well aware that Mr Mac had already hidden his own wireless set in the boiler house.

Shortly thereafter, my father accepted the opportunity to move us into one of two larger, newly-built houses on the St Clement Inner Road at La Blinérie on the sole proviso of being able to purchase the property after the war when the housing market returned to normal. Construction on the two houses had begun in 1939, shortly before the start of the war, and the builder was barely able to complete the development before all the Island's building supplies, especially concrete block and cement, had been requisitioned and taken over by the Germans.

Rather than give the house a proper name, my parents decided to leave it the way it was, No. 2, La Blinérie. Just up the lane from the beach at Green Island, it had a large front and back garden, plus a detached garage to the rear, which also included a large, built-in potting shed with a wide, frosted glass window. The potting shed would serve as a garden tool shed, carpentry shop, bicycle store, and later a place where I kept my four white mice.

One of the first things my father had to do upon moving us into the new house was to see that we had removable blackout blinds made for every window. The Germans had imposed a full night-time blackout across the Island on the strict understanding that they would shoot through any window that emitted even the smallest speck of light.

One day, as a precaution in the event of an air raid, my father brought home three steel helmets, each of them painted white. Two were British army helmets – one each for him and my mother – and a third, smaller-sized French army helmet with a badge on the front was for me. I would have preferred to have a British helmet like the others, but the French one fitted me perfectly and to prove that it would adequately serve its purpose, my father whacked the top with a hammer!

Next came the immediate task of cultivating every inch of the gardens in order to produce what had become the most important of all wartime commodities – food! However, my father also made sure to include enough space to sow a double row of half-concealed[4], and hopefully unnoticed, tobacco plants, the leaves of which he would harvest and hang up to dry and cure in

---

4 *The Germans strictly controlled the growing of tobacco and to do so required a special permit.*

the loft until it came time to roll and slice them up for his pipe. He also found space for a chicken coop and a row of rabbit hutches, and finally, but not least, my father had an air raid shelter dug and provisioned at the far end of the back garden.

At the same time, my father took the opportunity to hide his new crystal set and earphones inside a felt hat that hung on a peg in full view downstairs in the cloakroom. This was of course something I was unaware of, until a disturbing incident arose later on during the war.

Much to my delight, Nigel and his parents had also moved into a lovely detached house about 250 yards down from us on the Inner Road. The early 1940 evacuation to mainland Britain of all those who were not born in the Island had left many properties vacant and unattended. This may have been part of the reason why Nigel's parents were able to move into their new home, just across the road from the large meadow below the "front woods" where Samarés Manor pastured a huge Jersey bull that was tethered and pegged by two ropes attached to a brass ring through its nose.

Just across the Inner Road and opposite from our house was Beauvoir, another large house with a walled-in garden. The owner of this house, Commander Ainsley, had evacuated with his family to England shortly before the Germans had landed, leaving the property in the care of an elderly housekeeper and Francis Le Sueur, a young advocate turned local fisherman. Francis was imprisoned after having been caught trying to escape from the Island. In September 1944 he escaped from German custody and made a successful second escape from the Island to France. Consequently, the Germans commandeered Beauvoir and billeted

Francis Le Sueur

troops there, while at the same time allowing the housekeeper to remain and continue with her duties. The Jerries treated Beauvoir with a fair amount of respect, and even left undisturbed the large stuffed Nile crocodile that spanned the floor of the main hallway.

Behind our house there was a gravel lane, with grassy patches running along its sides and down the middle, that led to the back of another large house. This is where Cyril Luce and his older sisters lived. Between our two houses there was an open field where Mr Mauger, after a long day's work at the Gasworks, would toil away with his teenage son in cultivating vegetables until shortly before nightfall, allowing just enough time for them to ride home before the curfew.

Cyril's father, Hedley Luce, was the Island's Solicitor General and was therefore very well acquainted with my grandfather. They were a devout Methodist family who, when at home, spoke nothing but our ancient Jersey-French patois amongst themselves. Because my mother had come from England as a young girl to live in Jersey with her family, I became one of many in a generation that would grow up with English as my first language, although as early as three years old at Mandalay we were taught "proper-French!"

On the north side of the grassy gravel lane behind our house, there was a large field farmed and cultivated by a very fat Frenchman named Bottice Callec. The field sloped up to the north and was bounded by a long gravel driveway leading uphill to two houses that were both occupied by a detachment of German troops. Situated on the far side of the gravel driveway were the "back woods", in which the Jerries had laid a number of mines in order to guard the approaches leading up to a large calibre gun that was hidden inside an octagonal hut overlooking a quarry. It would be at the bottom of the long gravel driveway where I would come to know Fritz the guard on the days when he stood sentry duty.

Cyril Luce, or Zuggie as we knew him, was a year or so older than me. He and his sister Elizabeth were in Miss Garnier's upper classroom at Mandalay. My mother made arrangements so that we would all leave and walk to school together in the morning, picking Nigel up on the way. To mark the first occasion, my mother took a picture of us before leaving, using the last remaining negative in her Kodak Box Brownie camera before it was turned in to the German authorities who had banned all civilians from owning and using cameras.

Very often, on our way to school, we would meet a company of passing German soldiers marching towards us in ranks of three with rifles sloped, singing their Nazi Party songs. One of their marching songs was called *Ein Heller und ein Batzen*, (meaning "A Penny and a Farthing") which had such a rousing chorus, known as *I-E-I-E-I-O*, that it became so familiar to everyone that most of the kids on the Island would join in until the Jerries had passed by, when we would all come back at them with:

Whistle while you work, Mussolini is a twerp,
Hitler's barmy, so's his army, whistle while you work!

One day, while we dawdled our way home from Mandalay school, the word "actually" suddenly popped up into my mind. I had absolutely no idea what it meant, but loved its sound and ravished the adult feeling it gave to me when articulating the word from the back of my mouth. It was a grown up word, one that had just popped up from somewhere within me. As Cyril spoke both Jersey-French and English, I asked him if he knew what "actually" meant, but he didn't. Elizabeth, Cyril's sister, said it meant nothing and that I was too young to be thinking of such words. Nevertheless, "actually" became my first grown-up word and I loved being able to say it just like any adult – regardless of what it meant.

~   ~   ~

Shortly after we settled in at La Blinérie, the Germans discovered that someone had cut their telephone lines to the north of the back woods. The Nazis ordered Mr Cyril, our local parish Connétable, the head of the parish, to detail enough local men to guard the German field phone wires around the clock for two weeks. As a result, my father found himself numbered amongst those who ended up doing several bouts of all-night guard duty after a long day at work.

Later, in September 1942, *Feldkommandant* Knackfuss informed the Island's Bailiff, Alexander Coutanche, and the Superior Council, of Hitler's order for the deportation to Germany of all British nationals who were not born in the Island. This came as a profound shock to the Superior Council, causing the Bailiff to forward an immediate official protest to Knackfuss, accompanying it with the threat of the Council's resignation. However, Lt Col Baron von Aufsess, the officer who was second in command under Dr Casper, the Chief Administrator of *Feldkommandantur* 515, quietly advised the Bailiff and my grandfather on the council that it would be better for the Islanders in the long-run if the Governing Council remain in place as it was.

By the end of September, 1,186 deportees from Jersey found themselves rounded up and shipped off to Germany, with similar numbers from Guernsey, Alderney and Sark. Many Islanders quickly got together to collect food, clothing, footwear and whatever they could afford to give the deportees in order to provide for their uncertain journey and ordeal. Amongst those rounded up was one of my classmates, Peter Cardnell, who was the same age as me, and his mother, who was a close friend of my parents. My mother took what would be the last box of French sugar cubes that we would see for a long time, and gave it to Peter's mother so that she would have something sweet with which to comfort her son on the long impending journey.

The thought of being sent away to Germany at that time was very frightening for me – would Peter and his mum be all right? What would happen to them? When would they return? I asked my father to tell me where Germany was, and he pointed to the north-east and said it was over and beyond Grumpa's house, across the sea and across miles of foreign lands to the east. When I asked him to show me on the map, he pointed his finger to a large, dark green area, but this gave me no sense of the place from which these soldiers occupying our Island had come, or where my friend Peter would be going. I remember looking at it for a long moment before turning away. Somehow, it had all become too much for me to take in – I would go and see how the rabbits were doing in their hutches outside.

~ ~ ~

5 Grumpa's house

As Christmas 1942 drew near, my parents decorated the dining room, and as I eagerly waited for Father Christmas to come, I worried whether or not the Jerries might try to shoot him down before he could reach our chimney pot. However, my father kindly reassured me that Father Christmas and his sleigh could fly faster than any German Messerschmitt, or a British Spitfire for that matter, and the noisy German anti-aircraft guns with their powerful searchlights could not catch him even if they tried!

On Christmas morning I ran into the playroom and sure enough, there under the tree sat a huge, freshly painted wooden fortress, complete with a drawbridge, a central keep, parapets, walls with corner towers and crenellations! It was magnificent! How Father Christmas managed to get it down the chimney was a mystery far beyond me. Little did I know that this lovely present was the main reason why my father had kept the potting shed door locked in the daytime during the month or so leading up to Christmas, while he modelled the fort out of wood that he had salvaged from some old potato boxes.

My father had also managed to secure a second-hand, French-made ladies' bicycle for my mother. It was light brown and had solid rubber puncture-free tyres that did not require inner tubes. He had had a wicker basket seat with straps fitted onto the rear for my sister Diana, and together, with me on the crossbar of his bike, we all set off on a cold crisp morning for Grumpa's house at Arquerondel, known today as Archirondel, where we and other members of our family would spend the Christmas holidays in the warmth and comfort of Anneville Lodge.

Once my mum and dad had pushed their bikes to the top of the hill below Nicolle Tower, which had been turned into a German lookout post surrounded by mines with *Achtung Minen!* signs warning to stay clear, we continued our ride along the narrow winding country lanes towards Grumpa's house. We passed the heavy calibre anti-aircraft gun battery and searchlights that were unable to catch Father Christmas on the previous night. Not too long after, we passed two Jerry guards sheepishly standing watch outside the barbed wired gates to the hutted internment camp where some of the forced workers and Russian prisoners would be spending what would surely be a miserable Christmas season.

Grumpa's house, Anneville Lodge

For my part, I can only describe Anneville Lodge as one of the most magical places on earth, and it remains so to this day. It was the only place in my entire little world where I could play and wander about without missing any of my friends. A grassy pathway led up through the bracken and past the summer flowering rhododendrons of the wooded *côtil*[5] above the lodge, past the camouflaged shed where Grumpa kept our two goats hidden from being requisitioned by the Jerries, and on up to the tall cedars overlooking the bay – my "secret place of the most high."

From my secret place, I could also look down and see the granite farmhouse just above the sea wall at Arquerondel where Ralph Ferrait, who was my age, lived with his parents. The Ferraits farmed and grew summer wheat in the huge field that ran all the way across the bay. Later during the war, when I would stay with my grandparents for a couple of weeks during the summer school holidays, Ralph and I would play together on the safe upper mine-free area of the pebbled beach where we could paddle around in the water at high tide. Of all the kids I knew, Ralph had the toughest feet in the world. He could run across the stones and rocks faster than anyone.

I would love to sit on the soft carpeting of pine needles beneath a towering cathedral of cedar trees where I could look all the way out, some fourteen miles across the sea, to the coast of Normandy. At the same time, I could hear the sound of the natural waterfall in the front garden below and listen to the

---

5 *Jersey-French (Jerriais) for hillside — either natural or cultivated.*

bubbling water as it flowed along a shallow brook towards two large ponds at the end of the garden. Every two years, my grandfather would hang a couple of fishing lines from the little arched bridge that separated the two ponds so that he could catch some of the big meaty eels that would have migrated from the Sargasso Sea, in which they were spawned. I asked Grumpa why it was that the eels would want to travel so far in order to live and grow in our ponds.

"It's because of some special magic spirit in the water." He explained. "It's said to come all the way from the Pyrenees Mountains of Spain. It's what gives the growing eels the secret power to guide them all the way to back to the Sargasso Sea so they can breed and spawn in the waters where they were born."

One thing about Grumpa that I never quite got over was the fact that all the answers he gave to my questions would always stimulate a mountain of thoughts and produce a huge sackfull of new questions – like what kind of magic lived in the water?

From the top of the point I could also see the rotating Flack 29 Oerlikon gun, which the Germans had installed atop the eighteenth-century Conway tower that overlooked both Archirondel beach, including Ralph's farm house, and all the way out across St Catherine's bay to the end of the long breakwater. Throughout most of the Island's beaches, the Germans had set lots of limpet mines and anti-tank barriers that in turn were overlooked by massive concrete bunkers, some of which were cunningly concealed, camouflaged and capable of inflicting a devastating amount of fire power upon whatever might dare attempt any kind of invasive landing.

Uncle Edward, my grandfather's youngest brother, arrived on his bicycle shortly after we did. He lived at Hamptonne, where he had been born. It was an eighteenth-century family property in Le Hocq Lane with several cottages attached to it and was no more that a short walk from where we lived at La Blinérie. Hamptonne was one of four large family farms, three of which belonged outright to my grandfather, which he leased out to tenant farmers.

The farms included La Davisonerie, which had been in the family since 1600.[6] Then there was Temple View, an early nineteenth-century property that overlooked the ancient dolmen[7] at Faldouet, where Grumpa himself was born. And finally there was Anneville Farm itself, dating back to the early seventeenth century, whose fields bordered the top of the *côtil* overlooking the lodge where Grumpa and I would go in search for mushrooms in the late afternoons before supper.

The Germans granted my grandfather and others serving on the Special Council permission to keep and drive their cars on a limited ration of petrol.

---

6 *Where Sir Hugh Paulette had once lived somewhere around the 1580s when Governor of Jersey.*
7 *Dolmen – La Pouquelaye de Faldouet – Megalithic tombs – "stone table" in Breton.*

They also allowed some of our local doctors, including Dr Lewis, our family doctor, to keep and drive their cars under similar conditions. Therefore, while my parents and grandma were busy preparing the Christmas meal in the kitchen and decorating the table in the dining room, Grumpa got in his car and went to pick up his sister, Auntie Nan and Auntie Maud-Anna, his brother Anquetil's widow.

Uncle Anquetil, acting major in the Canadian 7th British Columbia Regiment, had fallen in action in France 1917 during the famous battle of Vimy Ridge. His son, Uncle Bill, whom I only knew at that time through pictures shown to me by Auntie Maud-Anna, was away fighting the Germans in some distant part of the world. After the war, having been highly decorated, he took the exclusive command of the King's Troop of the Royal Horse Artillery and eventually rose to the rank of brigadier.

I could always rely upon Uncle Edward to come up with a fantastic, grown-up Christmas present. That year he surprised me with a six-inch Boy Scout sheath knife! It was a real stabber! And I couldn't wait to show it to my friends – or the day when I would be old enough to go to Victoria College Prep School and be able to join the Eleventh Jersey Cub Scouts, which was run by Vernon Cavey, Titch Cavey's older brother.

"Oh he's much too young for that!" cried my mother.

"Nonsense!" replied Grumpa, promptly putting the issue to rest and presenting me with a lovely wooden sword that he had made in his workshop. It was an exact scaled-down replica of my great-great grandfather's militia sabre that hung upstairs behind the door in his office. However, my one-eyed grandma with her black pirate's patch topped the day when she presented me with a box of her homemade chocolate fudge! No one dare ask how she managed to find the necessary ingredients. All the toyshops and corner sweetshops had closed down long ago, and the only kind of sweets and things like bananas and oranges that were available were those in the form of faded pre-war picture advertisements – but then my grandma knew how to make real fruit jelly out of seaweed.

With a fire roaring in the granite fireplace, we all gathered and sat around the dining room table. Looking at the table it might have been hard for anyone to believe that there was a war going on. As Grumpa said grace and gave thanks, a picture of Peter Cardnell and his mum and dad, rounded up and shipped to who-knew-where, and the prisoners in the huts we had ridden past that morning flashed through my mind, but at that age I didn't have the understanding, or even the capability, to explain what I felt – even to myself.

6   Riding on hosepipe tyres

The mile and a half walk to and from school each day may well have been seen as good exercise for us, but it was no longer as much fun, especially on cold January mornings. Cyril and his sister were no longer there to hurry us along and see that we arrived on time. Both had moved up to new schools, Cyril now rode a bike to Victoria College Prep each day – something which, as a six-year-old, I longed to be able to do myself, like all the older kids.

I remember being especially late one morning after Nigel and I had stopped by the stables situated just inside the entrance to Florence Boot Playing Fields. The Jerries had billeted some of their troops in the main building overlooking the football pitches and they had also stabled quite a few horses there, including a beautiful white frisky mare named Froni, a gentle horse named Toni, a dark, elegant horse named Satan, and Monarch, one of the tallest and most majestic horses we had ever seen.

A smartly-polished junior rank German officer approached us and, speaking in clear fluent English with barely any trace of a foreign accent, he pleasantly bid us a good morning. Forgetting all about school, we soon became engaged in light conversation, asking him lots of questions about what he liked, what he thought, whether he had any brothers or sisters, did he like football, had he ever played cricket, did he miss his mother and father? In addition, when asked what his favourite thing to eat was, he answered, "Strawberries and cream."

Nigel asked him if he had ever shot anyone with his pistol. To which he answered, "No!" Then picking up a small handsaw that someone had left on the wall by the entrance, he raised it to the side of his neck and pretending to saw away said, "No. I like to cut off little boys' heads when they are late for school!" Nigel and I ran.

Neither Miss Le Quesne nor Miss Garnier believed us when we told them that we had been stopped by a German who wanted to cut our heads off with a saw, so instead of being allowed to go out during the break, we were made to sit at our desks without talking. One thing in life that I was assuredly beginning not to enjoy was sitting in Miss Le Quesne's class!

Just before Christmas, the Germans had issued a very disturbing and ominous order, making it an offence for anyone not to report an infraction of German rules. Then, in the following February of 1943, the Germans ordered that all "unreliable elements" should be deported and interned in Germany. The list included any Jews, retired ex-army officers or former reservists, persons with previous convictions and, notably, any young men without useful employment. As a result, the Island saw another 201 people deported to Germany.

In March, the first series of arrests for having a wireless set saw nineteen men receive harsh sentences – four of them were deported to prisons in France, and from there to work camps elsewhere on the Continent.

Then, to make matters worse, the Germans, citing the Hague Convention, became intent upon requisitioning local labour – especially anyone who wasn't in what they considered to be "useful employment." The Superior Council immediately challenged the legitimacy of this order and a huge argument ensued between them and both Dr Casper and *Feldkommandant* Knackfuss.

Bob Sowden's father, a hardy old sea salt who captained the SS *Normand*, a coastal cargo vessel involved in transporting essential commodities to the Island, was imprisoned by the Germans for refusing to transport munitions aboard his ship from Granville to Jersey, and willingly accepted a term in prison rather than lift a finger to help the enemy.

In defence against such orders, the Council cited and insisted that international law excludes all work connected with operations against one's motherland. Nevertheless and needless to say, many men and women found themselves pressed, in some cases enticed by a higher wage, into working for the Germans. I knew one such man; he had to drive a grey-green Jerry army wagon drawn by two large imported workhorses. Whenever he came by, he would always stop and give us a lift either to or from school. One day, while riding up beside him on the wagon bench, I asked him why he worked for the Germans.

"Ah, the Jerries them, they don't give you no choice ay." he said. "When the buggers tell you to work, that's what you 'ave to do you," he explained. "Only, when they ain't looking, I just takes it a little bit slower than what they like ay."

In May, after the Allies had raided the shipping in and around the Channel Islands, the German OB West (military governor in France) threatened in reprisal to reduce all food rations across the Islands. The Superior Council immediately attempted an appeal to the International Red Cross via the Swiss Embassy in Berlin, but unfortunately it was to no avail. In the following three months the bitter taste of things to come began to dawn upon us when the

Islands were forced to suffer the additional shortages, which did no more than give rise to an increase in the black market activities that were emerging on both sides of the struggle. It was not until later in August, after the Germans had reconsidered their position, that they restored food rations to their former level.

Meanwhile, my father was heavily engaged in producing sugar beet syrup at the factory. Once the factory had run out of cans in which to seal and preserve food, and with no sugar supplies coming into the Island, the black sugar beet syrup they produced and bottled in recycled jam jars became the staple sweetener of the day. The Germans wanted my father to can meat for their troops. Fortunately for my father, the Germans immediately dismissed the idea when he explained to them that the Continental Can Company in Canada owned the factory's patented canning machinery. This meant that only a certain type and gauge of can, that the Jerries were unable to produce or supply, could be run through the production lines. In the meantime, my father persuaded the Germans to allow him to dig and build a large bomb shelter for his employees in the central garden roundabout. Uncle Edward, who for years had produced a good quality cider made from the apples in the orchard at Hamptonne, kindly helped to provision the shelter by carting in several cases of his best brew – brew that the Germans wouldn't get their hands on.

As the summer holidays from school drew near, my father surprised me with a lovely pre-war second-hand bicycle. It had silver handle bars and pump-up tyres with a saddlebag and carrier on the back. It was just what I had been so longing for, and was soon to become my ticket to roam. Unfortunately, the inner tubes in the tyres had suffered many prior punctures, like those on every other bike on the Island, and they were no longer replaceable. One had the choice of either riding on bare rims or taking a length of garden hosepipe and fashioning it into a homemade tyre. Most people would simply attach the hosepipe to their wheels by drilling a couple of holes through the rims and then bolting the ends of the piping together where they met. Nevertheless, my father told me to take my bike into the factory machine shop on the way to school and ask Mr Mac if he could work some of his special magic and see what he could do for me.

When I returned to the factory machine shop later that afternoon, Mr Mac's magic, to the amazement of everyone, including my dad, had indeed done its job. Mr Mac had taken some high-pressure factory hose and mounted it onto the rims of my wheels without so much as a trace of an ugly nut or bolt to hold it in place. The two ends of the rubber piping met perfectly in a seemingly invisible joint – and it was a very long time before anyone could ever find out how Mr Mac had done it. Very often, when my bike was parked somewhere, men and some of the older boys up at Victoria College, who couldn't believe their eyes, would stop and look to see if they could work out how Mr Mac had mounted the rubber hose tyres.

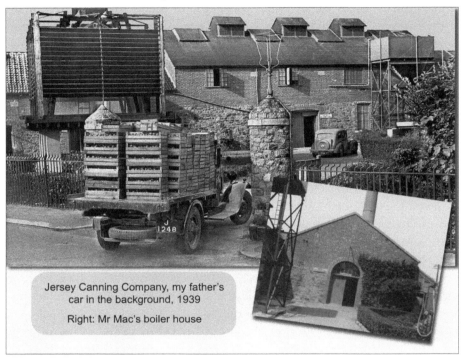

Jersey Canning Company, my father's car in the background, 1939

Right: Mr Mac's boiler house

One morning as I was about to hop on my bike for school, my mother came running out to stop me because my father had left his wallet on the telephone table in the front hallway. Having sealed it in a large brown manila envelope, she put it into my saddlebag and told me to drop it off at daddy's office on my way. Of course, this was a big mistake, because being who I was at that age I would have forgotten all about the wallet by the time I was half a mile down the road – which I did!

Later, when it came time for our play break in the gardens at Mandalay, I took the envelope containing my father's wallet out of my saddlebag and showed it to Nigel, Titch, Bob and Drelaud. Opening the wallet we found a number of large, dark blue, twenty Reichsmarks, Occupation bank notes. On the left of each note there was a mean-looking blue-tinted picture of Hitler with his little snotty moustache. Knowing how much my father hated Hitler and his bloody army, I offered the notes to my friends and anyone else who might like to have one – Drelaud took two, which I exchanged with him for a red Dinky toy car with one missing tyre.

After I had returned home and finished my homework that evening, a very upset Miss Garnier, having peddled all the way out to our house, knocked on the front door. Apparently, she had received several inquiries from a number of distraught parents, all wanting to know why their children had returned home from school with some rather large denomination Reichsmark notes – all of which their children had received from yours truly! Of course, my mum and dad were both furious with me! I thought for sure I was in for a right whacking! But, after explaining to my father why I had given his money away, namely because of the ugly, mean-looking pictures of Hitler on the notes in his wallet, as luck would have it, he chuckled and let me off – with a dire warning!

~   ~   ~

7   Prep and Miss Painter's ruler

September 1943 saw Titch, Bob, Drelaud and I enrolled for the autumn term at Victoria College Prep up in the De Carteret building at Mont Millais. I had just turned seven years old and was excitedly looking forward to joining Cyril and some of our older friends up at Prep. With virtually nothing readily available in any of the remaining shops and with everything from pins to putty on ration, my mother had spent most of the prior summer in acquiring whatever she could in order to get me properly outfitted for the new school.

Naturally, at that young age, none of us really understood the immense difficulties and the distressing toll of uncertainty that our parents had to endure, fuelled by the stringent ongoing food and fuel rationing. The wartime depravations and the annoying frustrations arising out of being unable to obtain even the most mundane of everyday items. Having to decide what to give in exchange for some tooth powder, a piece of soap, a candle, thread for sewing, paper and pencils for school, an old piece of leather to repair a pair of second-hand shoes, a lace curtain out of which to make underwear.

Somehow my mother managed to get hold of a blazer pattern and some blue thread for her hand-driven sewing machine, and salvaged material from one of my father's old college blazers to make me a new blazer for school. Grandma unpicked some old grey sweaters and knitted a warm V-necked school sweater for me, along with some new socks, all properly cuffed in the Prep colours.

Shoes had become all but impossible to obtain. To save what we had, except for Sunday school, we would run barefoot during the summer holidays. My father even removed the studs from his old hockey and football boots, polished them up with some harness dressing he found in the tack-room at Hamptonne, and wore them to work on cold rainy days. Even his old leather ski boots from the twenties would eventually find their use. I mention the harness dressing, because my father would have gone barefoot rather than use bartered German boot polish on any of his footwear.

Bicycling to school definitely had its ups-and-downs. No matter which route any of us would take – and there were several – getting there was always an uphill job. Generally, there was not very much motorised traffic on the

Island's roads. The Germans had commandeered most of the cars and then shipped them off to France, leaving the Island with all but a few essentially needed vehicles, including one or two buses, specially converted to run on large charcoal-burning tanks mounted on the rear end. Sometimes, with a bit of luck, we could hitch a lift by hanging onto the tailgate of a slow-moving lorry driving up to the top of Don Road, where we'd let go! That got one to the bottom of Mont Millais, where I would usually meet up with Drelaud and Titch Cavey.

Geoffrey, wearing his home-made Prep school blazer, early 1944

My friend Nigel was now at a different school, and except for playing together in the front woods above the bull field on weekends, I missed attending school with him.

Victoria College and its Prep was a traditional all boys' school with housemasters – generally an all male establishment. However, most of the younger male teachers had left at the beginning of the war to fight against Hitler. Therefore Prep ended up with a number of substitute female teachers. Miss Cassimir, a locally well-known professional educator, became the head teacher during the war, which was more than just fine as far as we were concerned, because unlike up at College, neither she nor Miss Aubrey, one of our other teachers, believed in caning – at least that is what they said! On the other hand, Miss Joan Painter, our new first-form teacher, who had recently left St Clement's Elementary School to join the staff up at Prep, had an entirely different attitude. While she may have been much prettier than Miss Le Quesne down at Mandalay, she could certainly be twice as strict, dare I say a little hard!

Her first disciplinary option was one to three whacks across palm and fingers of each hand with the sharp, thin side of a twelve-inch wooden ruler – and boy did it bloody hurt! For the more serious offence, her second option was to march us down to the storeroom at the back of the building, where she would dish out anywhere from three to six strokes on our backsides with the flat side of a three-foot brass tipped ruler. On my first visit to the backroom she sat down on a stool, ordered me to take off my coat, undo my braces and drop my trousers. At first, I thought she was going to put me over her knee as we had seen her do when she whacked Titch on the seat of his trousers up in the classroom.

However, on this occasion as I shuffled towards her with my trousers around my ankles, she suddenly stood up and said, "No, I want you to bend over that low bench with your hands down on the floor!"

Getting punished this way never seemed any more painful to me than getting whacked across my hands and fingers with the sharp side of her painful mean ruler upstairs in the classroom. The important thing that we had all agreed amongst ourselves was to remember to yell as loud as we could after each whack so as to pretend that it hurt a whole lot more than it really did, in the hope that she might back off on the next one!

~   ~   ~

During our first term up at Prep, the Island's Superior Council saw a shake up in the German High Command. *Oberst* (colonel) Rudolf Graf von Schmettow was promoted to rank of major general, replacing General Müller, who took on duties elsewhere in support of the German war effort in Europe. This meant that von Schmettow moved to Guernsey to take command at the Military HQ, where a hostile rivalry began to develop between the General and the Nazi hardliner, Vice Admiral Hüffmeier.

At the same time, Colonel Heine took over as Siege *Kommandant* in Jersey and Lieutenant Colonel Baron Max von Aufsess replaced Dr Casper and became the Chief Administrator for the Channel Islands. This, according to Grumpa, might well be better news for us.

Known and referred to by almost everyone, including those on the Superior Council, as "the Baron," von Aufsess was without doubt, a highly sophisticated German nobleman; a natural diplomat with impeccable manners. He was a lawyer by profession, loved the arts and was an author and ardent horticulturalist; von Aufsess took a deep and genuine interest in the Island's natural environment. He took particular delight in visiting the gardens at Samarés Manor and could often be seen galloping von Schmettow's lovely white mare, Froni, which remained stabled at the Florence Boot Playing fields, across the beach at La Mare.

The Bailiff, Alexander Coutanche, and Charles Duret Aubin, the Island's Attorney General, both found "the Baron" to be the preferred first line choice of communication when having to deal with the German military mind and the Nazi authorities within the occupying forces. While my grandfather, in his public capacity, respectfully recognized the Baron for the gentleman and diplomat that he was, he would politely refuse to shake hands with the

Nazi Admiral Hüffmeier, 1945

Major-General Graf
Rudolph von Schmettow
C-in-C Channel Islands
Commander 319 Infantry Division,
1940

Baron Max von
Und Zu Aufsess

Lt-Col Baron Max von Und Zu
Aufsess, 1944

man, making it very clear that the line of allegiance which existed between them would never be crossed. No matter how reasonable, sophisticated and polite von Aufsess may have been, at the end of the day, he was, as far as my grandfather was concerned, still the enemy!

One Sunday, during one of our rationed wartime luncheons at Anneville

Lodge, my grandfather expressed his profound disapproval regarding the behaviour of Alexander Coutanche. Apparently, on several occasions, the Bailiff and his wife had invited a number of senior German staff officers, including both von Aufsess and Lieutenant Colonel von Helldorf[8], into their home to discuss what was said to be "pressing wartime issues" over a glass of whisky – a precious pre-war luxury no longer available, not even on the black market.

"Good Scottish whisky for God's sake!" Grumpa angrily insisted. "And all in the name of what he claims to be 'our necessary administrative relationship!' Sometimes I believe the man is nothing more than a wily, self-absorbed politician at best!"

"Well I suppose he has to get along with the blighters somehow, Dad." reasoned my father, rather unexpectedly when considering how much he hated the Germans.

"True!" said my grandfather. "But, dash it all, you don't do it socially over a glass of British whisky!"

~   ~   ~

Around the beginning of November 1943, we learned from Miss Painter that the German field-police had arrested her father, Clarence Painter, and her two brothers Peter and John. The *Feldgendarmerie* were holding them after discovering a wireless, a camera, and worst of all, a WWI German Mauser pistol hidden in Peter's bedroom. A violation that could see anyone involved facing a firing squad. Fortunately, John Painter, Peter's younger brother, who was under eighteen and still attending Victoria College, was found to be uninvolved and released from custody. In the meantime, Peter and his father were in deep trouble.

Four days before Christmas, Peter and his father were deported to France from where they would be shunted on through a series of brutal concentration work camps and, little did anyone know at the time, never to return.

By the middle of the month, it began to get quite cold. Each morning when Miss Painter arrived, she would light the coal fire in the small classroom grate, which managed to take the chill out of the air and warm the room. Every so often, she would allow those who generally behaved and sat at the back of the classroom to get up and gather around the fire for a few minutes so that they might warm their hands. On the other hand, Drelaud, Titch and I, on permanent assignment to the front row, within easy reach of Miss Painter's ruler, had the warm satisfaction of being nearer to the fire.

---

8 *Lt Col. von Helldorf was ADC to General Graf von Schmettow.*

Miss Painter

Peter Painter

Clarence Painter

One of the things I most clearly remember about Miss Painter during class was that when we wanted to get her off the current work subject, we would ask her to show us pictures of her brother Peter dressed in his khaki British OTC (Officer Training Corps) uniform – something, that as little boys, we all aspired to wear one day. She kept the crinkle-edged snapshots in an envelope in her desk drawer and when asked, seldom refused to let us gather round and look through them.

Standing smartly in his OTC uniform on the college playing field just across the road to the north of our classroom, I can still see the sun-squinting smile upon Peter's face; a young Jerseyman nearing the end of his final term, ready and, like most young men of his age, eager to go out into the world beyond.

No doubt the names of Peter and his father will eventually fade from modern memory, but for a group of young seven-year-old boys, Peter Edward Painter served as a perfect role model. He had been an Eleventh Jersey Boy Scout troop Leader and a first-class sportsman who had distinguished himself both in the playground and on the field. His fine example stirred up a patriotic vision in our young imaginations, but for the time being we would have to wait until after the war in order to learn the tragic details of Peter and Clarence Painter's awful plight.

~   ~   ~

8   Help from a Jerry

By January 1944, the weather had become miserably cold. Titch, Nigel and I were suffering with badly chapped lips and all of us had developed painful chilblains on our toes and fingers. Titch could hardly hold his pencil to write in class. Drelaud got impetigo. Diphtheria was spreading with frighteningly fatal results throughout the population.

Dr Lewis, our family doctor and a friend of my parents, had a special permit to have a car, signed by Grumpa. One Sunday afternoon, he and his wife and baby son came to tea. After which I experienced my first injection with a blunt, reusable needle as Dr Lewis inoculated me against diphtheria! I felt tricked and quite hard done by – not the sort of thing one would normally expect during a social visit on a Sunday afternoon! Little did I understand at that time how lucky I was, because the recent increase in Allied air attacks over the Channel had drastically reduced the amount of critical supplies reaching the Island from France. Everything had become scarcer than ever, including desperately needed medicines.

Just a short time later, after Dr Lewis' Sunday visit and to make things worse, Diana, now two and a half years old, swallowed an open kirby grip, which promptly became stuck in her bowel! Dr Lewis was able to arrange for an x-ray, already in short supply, which thankfully showed that the sharp end of the kirby grip was pointing in an upward direction.

"She's too young for us to operate on." Dr Lewis declared. "Besides, the Germans have rationed all of our anesthetic and fine cat-gut for serious cases only! The only thing we can do at this time is to get some cotton wool down her throat and into her tummy. Hopefully, it will catch on the open pin and eventually pass its way through."

"How are we going do that?" my mother asked frantically.

"Take some cotton wool and soak it in sugar beet syrup or mix it up in her gruel and then get her to swallow it down," suggested Dr Lewis. "Not an easy task I know, but we have no other option."

I remember the difficult process my mother had to go through with Diana each morning at breakfast in order to get her to swallow the syrup-laced cotton wool – it just seemed to go on forever.

Finally, and much to everyone's relief, the kirby grip passed through Diana's system. Dr Lewis' cotton wool prescription had managed to do the job! Unbelievably, about two weeks later, Diana went and did the very same thing all over again – she swallowed another kirby grip and my mother had to repeat the whole trauma and process once more.

~ ~ ~

Except for weekends and during the holidays, life for us really began after school each day on our bikes, which gave us a ticket to roam and get into whatever trouble might happen to cross our paths. Playing in the barns and lofts down at Petit Menage Farm, where Victor Pallot and his two sisters lived, after school was always fun. Especially later in the year when they had stacked the summer hay up high behind the main house and we were allowed to climb up to the top and slide down. The general rule was for most of us to be home in time for supper, get our homework done and be in bed by eight.

One day in March, when the weather had warmed and the evenings had begun to draw out, Drelaud told us that the Jerries had parked some big tanks along the Esplanade near West Park. After school, we all rode down there to look at what was going on. When we arrived, some older boys between ten and eleven years old from a local elementary school were already there for the same reason – to see the tanks. There were several Jerry soldiers attending them and I remember looking up at one soldier who smiled back as he sat atop the turret of one the tanks. After a while, one of the older boys looking at the tanks came over to me and asked if he could try out my bike, so I let him.

"I'll just go up there and back, all right?" he said and took off. I watched as he rode my bike along the Esplanade. Eventually he turned around and headed back toward us. By this time Drelaud, Titch and Bob were ready to head home.

"I'll catch up with you." I said and watched as they all took off.

When the older boy returned with my bike he would not give it back to me.

"I just want to try it one more time." He said. "I won't take long." And before I could object he sped off!

The older boy was somewhat bigger than I was, so there was not too much that I could do to stop him. I soon began to realize that he did not intend to give me back my bike.

When the older boy returned from his fourth ride I grabbed hold of the handlebars, straddled the front wheel and demanded he get off. We struggled for a bit, and being on my own and with no help from anyone passing by, I began to get a little scared and worried.

"Hey you!" came a sudden shout from behind me. The older boy looked up, I turned and saw the soldier who had smiled at me from the top of the tank turret.

"You give him bike, *ja!*" ordered the soldier. "Not yours, *ja!*" Without taking his eyes off the Jerry soldier, the boy loosened his grip on the bike, slowly got off and, shoving the bike at me, walked back a couple of steps, then turned and walked away without a word. I got back on my bike and looked at the soldier before peddling off. He nodded and gave me a friendly wink with his eye.

"*Danke,*" I said, using one of my limited half-dozen words of German. "Thank you."

"*Ja bitte.*" he said with a friendly smile, and he waved as I rode away.

That night, shortly before dozing off to sleep, I thought about the friendly Jerry soldier and what might have happened if he hadn't helped me get my bike back. Not only would I have had to walk all the way home, but I would also have been very late home, with a mile and a half of explaining to do on top of it. The experience posed a paradox for me in the form of a friendly Jerry soldier who had recognized my dilemma and troubled to go out of his way to help me. I closed my eyes and left these confusing thoughts for another time.

The heavy anti-aircraft guns woke me up. I got out of bed and went over to the window, where I pulled back a corner of the blackout so that I could look up and see the searchlight beams criss-crossing back and forth across the dark skies. Between the massive gun blasts and bursting shells, I could hear the droning engines of Allied aircraft passing overhead. When I heard this happen for the first time it frightened me out of my wits, but as the Allied activity became more and more frequent, and with the Jerries opening up each time they passed over the Island, I had come to know that once the aircraft had passed and flown beyond their range, the anti-aircraft guns would stop. So, at that moment I was no longer focusing on the horror of war or the confusion I felt over the German soldier's humanity in helping me get my bike back, but rather on how many pieces of shrapnel I would be able to find and collect on my way to school the next morning!

~   ~   ~

Sadly, one morning when we arrived at school, Miss Cassimir announced that one of the older boys in the sixth class had fatally crashed his bicycle into the wall at the bottom of Mont Millais Hill. As a result, and from then on, a new school rule forbade us from riding our bikes down the long hill. This meant that we would have to ride home along the back lane and head down via Petit Menage, Victor Pallot's farm, or divert around past the quarry above Belvedere Hill and then on towards the top of Don Road and the main entrance to Howard Davis Park.

The head park keeper, a miserable old turd if ever there was one, spent most of his day sitting in a little brown hut hidden away next to the west wall of the park and set behind the many trees and shrubs that surrounded the central lawn. However, he was always ready to intercept and chase after us for riding our bikes through the park, something he said we were not supposed to do.

Situated diagonally across the street from the park's main entrance stood the old Ritz Hotel. Like most of the hotels on the Island, the Germans had commandeered it as a billet for their troops. Every afternoon at around four o'clock, when the weather was fine, some of the German officers billeted at the Ritz would take a leisurely stroll in the park, mostly in search of some brief flirtatious encounter with an off-duty German nurse or with some passing, uniform beguiled local Jersey girl.

"Jerry bags" with German officers, 1943

Over the course of five long years of Occupation, it was probably only natural that relationships of some sort were bound to develop between the handsome young men in uniform and a number of young local women – who after all interacted with each other every day.

For obvious reasons during the Occupation, "horizontal collaboration" could never have become acceptable. Simply because in war it is essential for those on both sides to realize that there is a clearly-defined line between "us and them" – and that those lines should never blur. But of course, human nature being what it is, inevitably, somewhere along the way, the lines will not only blur, but they will cross.

Yes there were definitely a few flirtatious "Jerry bags" running around town who would eventually have to bear their shame and suffer ostracism in one form or another, and reprisals after the war.

Luftwaffe officers, 1941

But if most of these wartime relationships were fuelled by lust mixed with a little favour, one or two were real and genuine in spirit, and not limited to rank-and-file soldiers – even General Schmettow's aristocratic adjutant, Lieutenant Colonel von Helldorf, would find himself deeply in love with a young local chambermaid!

~　　~　　~

Of all the German officers, my favourite to look at were the Luftwaffe Officers. Their bluish, decorated uniforms with a flying eagle on their right breast and polished riding boots just seemed to be smarter and more dashing than all the rest. Above all they were pilots and flew fighter planes, and that, for any seven-year-old such as myself, really seemed to make them different. I remember looking at one particular officer; I can still see him to this day. He looked striking, and although I knew he was a German, an enemy of everything we knew to be British and proper, yet I was overcome by a shameful, if not fearful, feeling of awe and reverential respect.

One day, after having persuaded Miss Painter to show us the snapshots of her brother in his British uniform, we headed for the statue of King George V, which stood facing west just inside the main entrance to the park. Titch, Sowden, Drelaud and myself walked to the north side of the great statue, set our bikes aside and lined up with the park entrance to our right, where we waited until we saw four or five lower rank Jerry officers stroll into the park.

"Attention!" shouted Drelaud. Dutifully, we all snapped to attention. The Jerries pulled up for a moment and chuckled amongst themselves while they observed what they took to be four little boys playing soldiers.

"Left turn!" shouted Drelaud, and again we all dutifully turned toward the statue of King George V.

"Rule Britannia!" he cried, and with that, we all looked up at the bronze king and smartly saluted!

For one brief moment, the Jerries just stood there in stark disbelief until realizing what we were up to. Whereupon they became furious and started heading towards us. Fortunately, we were able to grab our bikes and pedal like hell along the nearest path yelling "Rule Britannia!" as we fled for our lives.

Of course, the miserable old turd of a park-keeper was standing slap in the middle of the pathway waiting for us. Jamming our breaks on, we skidded and slowed enough on the gravel path to turn and follow Drelaud across the bordering flower bed onto the central lawn where we could pedal straight for the south entrance – knowing all along that we might have some serious explaining to do at school the next day.

~   ~   ~

9   Black bread

After our escape from the park, Titch and Sowden turned off and headed for home, leaving Drelaud and myself at the top of Dicq Road.

"Are you hungry?" asked Drelaud. I thought for a moment, wondering what he might have in mind, because we were usually hungry and were always interested in something to eat.

"Why?" I asked.

"Have you ever eaten black bread?" asked Drelaud.

"Black bread!" I exclaimed. "Don't be silly!"

"No! I'm not!" he replied. "Honest! It tastes good. Come on, follow me."

We pedalled down to the bottom of Dicq Road, turned left and rode across into the car park of the Demi Des Pas Hotel, which the Germans had taken over as a billet for their troops. Drelaud got off his bike and left it against the low wall.

"Wait here." he said, and ran across the car park to an open ground-floor window and called to someone inside. A German cook appeared in the window and, recognizing Drelaud, warmly greeted him. After a few words, during which Drelaud had turned and pointed me out to the man, the cook disappeared for a moment and then returned with two large pieces of black bread, which he handed to Drelaud.

I had never seen, let alone ever imagined, such a thing as black bread.

"Go on, try it," said Drelaud after having handed me a piece. "It's good, you'll see!"

The bread certainly tasted different – different to anything I had ever known. Moreover, to be honest, it did taste all right – despite being an unfamiliar German type of taste at that – we gobbled down the treat. The next morning when Titch and I arrived at school, the head teacher, Miss Cassimir, was waiting outside her study in the main hallway with Drelaud, whom she was holding on to by his right ear.

"Norman!" she yelled as soon as she saw me. "Come here at once!"

I could tell by the look on her face that she was hopping mad about something! Immediately, I thought of the park keeper – the old turd had no doubt turned us in for riding across the flowerbed and the lawn. Miss Cassimir grabbed me by the ear and said nothing to Titch, who was right behind me, allowing him to continue up to our classroom wondering what was up.

"Into my study!" she ordered, "both of you – now!" Just then, Miss Painter came by and Miss Cassimir turned to her and said, "You come in, I want you to hear this."

We stood in front of her desk while Miss Painter waited to one side.

"Where did you go after school yesterday?" she demanded of me. Not sure what to say, I glanced at Drelaud for a moment.

"We went to play in the park." I replied

"And after that?" she inquired.

"We went down to Dicq Beach, near Demi Des Pas." I said.

"Really – down to Dicq Beach you say?" she queried. "Really! Well, young man, I received a note this morning from someone I know who lives in that area, who saw both of you taking bread from one of the German cooks at the Demi Des Pas Hotel! Is that right?"

Drelaud and I looked at each other. "What's so wrong with that?" I questioningly thought, "Kids talk to Jerries all the time."

"He just gave it to us." explained Drelaud. "We didn't steal it or nothing."

"That is not the point!" said Miss Cassimir, almost shaking with rage! "We don't beg bread from the Germans! Do you understand! It is not what we British do! Understand!"

Obviously, this was not going to be a good day for us – but dash it all, it just did not seem as if we had done anything that bad.

"Whose idea was this anyway?" she demanded. "Who told you to go there and ask for bread in the first place?"

Shifting slightly, Drelaud glanced at me for a moment before answering. "Mine," he admitted.

"All right!' said Miss Cassimir, getting up from her desk, "I'll speak to your parents about this. In the meantime I'm going to let Miss Painter deal with you!" With that, she headed out of the door, leaving us to the mercy of Miss Painter.

Of course, this ended with a visit to the back storeroom, where Drelaud got six for suggesting the idea and I got three for being stupid enough to listen to him! Overall it was better than getting a whacking from my dad when I got home. However, when my father found out about the incident, he merely patiently explained that we all had to draw and hold a line between the Germans and ourselves and never cross it.

"Even though one or two of them may seem friendly and nice to you," he explained, "they are still our enemy!"

~   ~   ~

On Sundays, I had the choice of either going to St Clement's church where I could sit and carve my initials into the family pew during the sermon, or I could go to Sunday school at the Methodist Chapel in La Hocq Lane with Cyril and his family. It was not so much that my parents were overly religious like Cyril's were; rather it had more to do with getting me out of the house on a Sunday morning so that they could get on with whatever else it was they

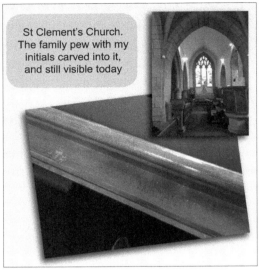

St Clement's Church. The family pew with my initials carved into it, and still visible today

needed to do. The Methodist Chapel, which they called Bethel, was located just across the lane from Hamptonne, where Uncle Edward lived and farmed the land, and where we would gather as a family once or twice a month on Sunday afternoons for tea. Sometimes, after learning a Sunday school text and singing a hymn or two with all the other kids, I would go across the lane and visit Uncle Edward or Old Marie, his Breton housekeeper, or see what Old Maurice and Charlie, Uncle Edward's farmhands, were up to in the stables, before walking home to La Blinérie for lunch.

From time to time Cyril, who was a couple of years older than I was, would play with Nigel and me in the front woods above the bull field. Moreover, Cyril hammered and nailed the first cross-boards of our tree house floor into place. Eventually, when finished and roofed, the tree house was able to hold and hide three of us at a time. From its slit window overlooking the upper part of Samarés Lane behind our house, we could see as far as Victoria College, our Prep school, up on the skyline, and College House at the far end of the playing fields, where Baron von Aufsess and *Feldkommandantur* 515 had established their main offices. Occasionally the Jerry soldiers, walking to and from their billets above Callec's field, would stop and look up at our tree house suspiciously for a moment, as though it might hold some unforeseen tactical threat in the event of an Allied invasion.

When enough of us gathered near the monkey tree in the front woods, a place where we liked to climb and play around, we could form two teams of roughly balanced sides made up of bigger and smaller kids. Sometimes, depending upon who was there, we would either play soldiers or drop down into the bull field and play football with an old leather ball stuffed with straw. Everyone knew that it could be very dangerous to enter any field in which a Jersey bull was grazing.

The Jersey bull

While the Jersey milk cow is quite a sweet and docile animal, the Jersey bull, on the other hand, is quite the opposite. Even when tethered by two ropes attached to a ring through its nose, the Jersey bull is nothing less than a flat out killer – an animal with which one should never trifle! However, there was one distinct advantage in defiantly deciding to play football in the bull's field – there were no cowpats! While playing in the other pastures where the cows grazed was sensibly safer, it always meant that someone, at some point when least expected, was bound to step into a slimy cowpat inevitably leading to cow dung being kicked all over the place! The only time it ever played into anyone's advantage was when there was enough cow poop on the ball that the goalkeeper would try to avoid touching it with his hands, thereby allowing one the increased possibility of scoring!

One day when we were playing in the bull field, Miss White, the manor's head housekeeper, who was in charge of the estate during the owner's absence, appeared by the gate at the other end of the field. Gathered with her on that occasion were some senior staff officers including Baron von Aufsess.

Lady Knott, the owner of the manor, was away in England when the Germans occupied the Islands in 1940. Later, in 1941, *Oberst*[9] Graf von Schmettow

9 *Oberst (Colonel) Rudolph Graf von Schmettow – Military Commander of the Channel Islands - later promoted to major general.*

commandeered the manor with its lavish gardens for the sole use of the high command staff. Although no senior staff officers ever billeted themselves at the manor, they did use it and its facilities as a sort of daytime retreat where they could meet and relax. Miss White had little choice other than to comply with the situation or choose, in the way that Bob Sowden's father had done, not to cooperate with the Germans and face the consequences. At the end of the day, Miss White chose to cooperate with the Germans, having convinced herself that in doing so she was primarily serving the best interests of both her mistress and the manor – similar, in some respects I suppose, to the Bailiff sharing a glass of whisky with senior German staff officers while discussing Island affairs.

Samarés manor

Nevertheless, in the absence of her mistress, Miss White promptly took advantage of her situation, which enabled her to hobnob with most of the senior staff officers. The result was that Miss White, as acting "lady of the manor", not only enjoyed privileges such as receiving first-hand information – albeit from a German perspective – it also meant an extra food ration here and there, including one or two rare delicacies such as might only be available on the black market. Thus, Miss White regularly and enthusiastically entertained her visiting staff officers by serving them afternoon tea in the drawing room or by accompanying them on a relaxing walk through the manor gardens.

"Get out of the field!" she cried, waving her arms in the air when she saw us playing. "You boys know you're not supposed to play there! Get out of there now!"

Seeing all the Jerry officers lined up beside her brought our play to a quick stop. One by one we all headed for the low wall at the foot of the front woods. Miss White and the officers waited until we had all cleared the field. Then, as Miss White and the officers began to turn away, Drelaud stepped back into the shadows of the woods behind us.

"Jerry bag!" he shouted at the top of his lungs. "Dirty old Jerry bag!"

The rest of us immediately turned and ducked back out of sight into the woods and began yelling every imaginable "Jerry bag" epithet contained within our rude playground vocabulary.

It may have been unfair of course, and we were not fully aware of all the implications of that epithet. I did have some guilty feeling about Miss White and the way in which we had treated her. After all, she had probably been more concerned about our safety in regards to the bull rather than trying to impress the Jerry officers. I decided I would keep it to myself.

~　　~　　~

10   Fritz the guard

Each morning as I set out for school on my bike I would pass the guard on duty at the bottom of the long driveway leading down from the two houses where the Jerries were billeted. The driveway exited onto Samarés Lane, just across from the house and from where Major Mourant lived with his wife and two very attractive teenage daughters. Most of the time the guards, who rotated on duty, either ignored or hardly took any notice of me as I passed by. After all, I was no more than a seven-year-old kid on my way to school.

Then one day as I rode by, the guard on duty smiled, nodded his head and said, "*Guten Morgen.*"

"Morning." I replied and shyly pedalled on. It was strange, I thought, how some of their German words sounded very similar to ours, while others, especially those that were very long and seemed to go on forever, sounded quite untranslatable.

A few days later after school on a Friday afternoon, while approaching the bottom entrance of the long driveway on my bike, I saw this same guard standing on duty again.

"Hello," he said with a friendly smile. "*Von schule kommen, ja?*"

Roughly understanding his question, I pulled up and straddled my crossbar. "Yes," I said nodding affirmatively. "From school."

"*Meine namen ist Fritz.*" he said. "*Mir Fritz, ja. Und sie? Ah, moment bitte.*"

Fritz adjusted the rifle slung on his shoulder and raised his finger so that I should wait for a moment. Searching through one of his tunic pockets, he pulled out a little red matchbox-sized German-English dictionary and quickly thumbed through its pages until he found the word he was looking for.

"*Ah hier,*" he said, pointing to a word. "*Hier ja.*"

I looked and saw that it was the word "your". "Your," I said.

"*Ah, 'your.'*" He repeated, and thumbed through more of the little pages. "*Moment bitte. Ah hier! Your Namen!*"

"Name." I said.

"*Ah. Namen, name,*" he repeated. "Your name?"

"Geoffrey," I answered. "My name is Geoffrey."

"*Ah Jeffie!*" he repeated. "*Ja gut – Jeffie! Mich…*" he continued pointing to himself, "*mich*, me, Fritz – mine name *ist* Fritz!"

"Fritz." I said.

"*Ja Fritz*," he replied with a broad smile. "Your name – *Jeffie ja*. Mine name Fritz!"

I nodded, "Yes, Geoffrey," I said.

"Hello Jeffie!" said Fritz happily with a broad smile. I saw that he had blue eyes, just like mine, and similar to those of my father.

Unslinging his rifle he sat down on the granite steps leading up into the back woods, and began to thumb through his little red dictionary again until he found another word he was looking for.

"*Mitkommen,*" he said.

I got off my bike and parked against the wall of Major Mourant's house.

"*Ah, hier bitte?*" he said, pointing out a particular word for me to look at. "*Abzeichen?*"

I looked at the word "*Abzeichen*" and saw that it translated as "badge or medal".

"Badge." I said.

"*Ja*. You like badge?" he asked.

"*Ja*. Yes I like," I answered.

"*Ja. Ich eine haben für sie*," said Fritz, pulling an Infantry Assault Badge out from his pocket and handing it to me.

I slowly turned the weighty solid-feeling badge over in my hand. It was a beauty – one that I knew that no one else had collected yet. As I began to hand it back to him, he put his hand up to stop me.

"*Nein! Nein!*" he said, shaking his head. "*Das ist für* – for you, *ja*. *Sie haben* – you have."

For a moment, I was not sure what to do. I certainly wanted to have the badge and could not wait to show it to all my friends, but I also knew that if my dad ever found out that I had taken something from a German, he would wring my neck!

"*Danke,*" I said. "Thank you."

"*Gut,*" said Fritz. "For you, *ja*."

The sound of an approaching vehicle immediately caught Fritz's attention. He looked up, listened for a moment and, recognizing a familiar sound, he quickly shouldered his rifle and went over to the field phone-box while I gathered my bike and straddled it. Fritz opened the box, took out the receiver and wound the handle. He waited for a moment then spoke to someone up in one of the billet houses. When he had finished, Fritz closed the box, straightened his tunic and, glancing in the direction of the approaching vehicle, quickly returned to his duty.

"Thank you Fritz," I said as I began to pedal off with the badge safely tucked away in my trouser pocket. "*Danke,*" I called back to him.

"*Wiedersehen Jeffie,*" he called and waved goodbye to me as I headed for home.

~   ~   ~

Bottom of the long driveway where Fritz stood guard

Major Mourant's house

May Colley, a kindly lady whom I had always known as Auntie May, and her daughter Elizabeth were visiting my mother when I arrived home after my encounter with Fritz. Elizabeth's father was away in England fighting in the war effort. Like Nigel Meeks, I had known Elizabeth, who was three years older than I was, for about as long as I could remember. After saying hello to everyone, my mother told me to go up to the playroom and get my homework done before my dad arrived home for supper.

"What's for supper?" I asked.

"Never mind," answered my mother, "just go and get your work done."

"I'll come up and help you with it, if you like," offered Elizabeth.

I readily accepted her offer and together we headed for the playroom.

Elizabeth, who took to schoolwork and did well in her class, was a perfect godsend that day, as I had a whole pile of sums, multiplications and divisions to do, and was desperately in need of some halfway decent marks on my worksheet. Neither Drelaud, Titch nor myself, who all sat together at the bottom of the class within reach of Miss Painter's ruler, were ever that enthusiastic about our academic studies, not when comparing them to running around and mucking about outside.

While I was far too young in those days to know anything about the birds and bees of life, I was without doubt very fond of Elizabeth. She wasn't like any of the other girls within a year or two of our age. Nor was she a tomboy or anything like it – in fact just the opposite. She was just a girl with long pigtails who seemed to fit in with whatever games and gang activities we got up to, be it football in the bull's field, or playing cowboys or soldiers in the front woods, where she would play the nurse and take care of the wounded. She simply enjoyed mucking about with us, and Elizabeth and I always seemed to end up playing on the same team.

~   ~   ~

Through Elizabeth's help and efforts I managed to get a nine out of ten score on the following Monday morning, and as a result at the end of the week I moved up two places in class so that I was now sitting directly in front of the fireplace. The only problem was that the weather had warmed up and a fire was no longer needed in the mornings, so I would have to wait until the weather got cold again in order to get the full benefit of my new position. Not to mention the fact that I would either have to remain in Elizabeth's good books or stay on my toes and do some real work in order to hold on to the same place.

Later that evening as I got ready for bed, I pinned the Infantry Assault Badge that Fritz had given to me onto my sweater and looked at myself in the mirror. Would I keep the badge as part of my collection or would I swap it for something else at school? What I really wanted was a Jerry forage cap with the eagle badge and the red, white and black button on the front, just like the one worn by Fritz. His would do very nicely. I pondered whether he might have a spare cap, one he might be willing to swap – there had to be something he might want. A thousand conniving thoughts began to pass through my mind until my mother stuck her head around the door to say goodnight.

"Did you say your prayers?" she asked.

"Yes," I replied. "I just finished and sent them off!"

~   ~   ~

11   Foot in a boot

"Geoffrey! Quick, get up! Quick, come and see!" she cried. "The Jerries have gone and shot down a plane!"

It may have been close to midnight when my mother came running into my bedroom. Normally I would have already awakened to the sounds of anti-aircraft fire and gone to the window, but on this occasion, I had slept all the way through the event. I got out of bed and followed my mother in the dark to my parent's bedroom, where my father was standing in the bay window looking out through a pair of binoculars.

Immediately I saw a ball of flame crossing the night sky and could hear the droning sound of spluttering engines mixed with a crackling, pop-popping noise.

"Is it one of ours?" I asked my father.

"No I think it's a Jerry plane," he answered. "Sounded like a Heinkel or a Dornier. I think the silly blighters may have gone and shot down one of their own!"

"What's that popping noise?" I asked

"Probably its engines conking out," he said

"No," I said. "The other noise, the crackling, pop-popping noise?"

"Probably their onboard ammunition exploding from the heat of the fire," he explained.

"What about the pilot?" I asked.

"If he hasn't already jumped, then I'd say his chances of survival are pretty thin," he said, shaking his head slightly. "Even if he is a bloody Jerry – not a nice way to go!"

The next morning being a Saturday with no school, Nigel and I hurried down Samarés Lane, heading towards the open fields just across the coastal road from Rockberg and Brian Harrison's house, and there we found the burnt-out wreckage.

There was not too much left of the aeroplane. All the trees near the crash site along the south side of the field, where the aircraft had come to rest, had been burnt or badly charred. Several kids, including Freddie[10] and his brother

---

10 *Freddie and Paul – not their real names.*

Paul, who lived in one of the old railway cottages near the parish elementary school, had already got there before us and were busy poking through the wreckage looking for anything to collect as souvenirs. So was Brian Harrison, his younger "tattletale" brother Gerald and their light brown Labrador mix dog.

Looking about, we found several burst cartridge casings lying amid the ashes, but Titch was the first among us to find anything of value. After lifting up a piece of twisted fuselage, Titch uncovered two live rounds of what we imagined to be machine-gun ammunition.

"Look!" he said to me, quickly grabbing them before any of the older boys saw what he had found, "and they're live ones!"

"Beauties," I said.

"I'll swap them for that new badge you just got." Titch suggested.

"No. I just got it." I said. "I don't want to swap it yet."

"Then hide them for me in your shed or in the tree house."

"Why? Don't you want them?" I asked.

"Yes I want them," said Titch. "But if my dad ever found out he'd kill me!" said Titch.

"So would mine," I said.

"Yes, but you have more places to hide them at your place than I do – look after them until we can find something to swap for them," he concluded, handing me the rounds.

"Hey! What you got there you?" demanded Freddie, who had moved in to see what was going on between us.

"Titch just found a couple of live bullets." I said, putting the rounds in my pocket.

"Let me see," asked Freddie.

"Why?" I asked.

"I'll swap them with you," said Freddie.

"They're Titch's – not mine," I said.

Freddie was older than the rest of us, and not someone we played with, and I knew that if ever he got his hands on the bullets, neither of us would ever see them again.

"I'll swap you for this," said Freddie, looking at Titch and holding up a piece of junk metal that he had just scavenged from the wreckage.

"What's that?" asked Titch, scratching and smoothing back his flop of ginger hair.

"It's the inside of a Jerry hand grenade," answered Freddie.

"How do you know?" asked Drelaud, joining the discussion.

"Because it is," said Freddie flatly.

"Don't be stupid, Titch," said Nigel. "He's only trying to trick you."

"If it was a real piece of hand grenade," said Brian Harrison, stepping in to even things up physically. "It would have exploded into a million little pieces."

"Yeah! A million pieces!" echoed Drelaud.

Freddie looked about and, realizing he had little in the way of support, decided to back off and join his little brother Paul who was busy trying to lift a piece of torn fuselage out of the scorched hedgerow.

With Freddie out of the way, the rest of us all went back to scrumping about the burnt-out wreckage in search of whatever else we might find. It was then that I noticed a piece of partially burnt parachute which I lifted up and was about to examine when I realized that it had been covering a boot – a boot with a man's foot that had been burnt off just above the ankle still inside it!

"Look at this!" I cried.

"It's a piece of parachute – I seen that already." said Freddie.

Remains of the bullet-riddled tail section of the Heinkel, as seen today in the Jersey War Tunnels museum

"No, down there. At the boot!" I said pointing to the slightly buckled boot. "Look, it's still got a foot inside it!"

I dropped the piece of parachute, picked up the boot, and immediately felt surprised by how heavy it felt.

"Let me see," said Drelaud, holding out his hand.

I passed the boot over to him and he too noted how heavy it felt before passing it over to Titch, who in turn passed it on until everyone had taken a look and it came back to me.

"Perhaps we can get it out." I suggested.

"You're mad, you!" said Freddie. "What you want to do with a dead Jerry's foot?"

I walked over to a patch of clean grass and sat down with the boot. Nigel, Titch, Drelaud and some others all followed and we began to undo the leather lacing. Eventually, after quite a struggle, we managed to get the foot out of the boot.

Sitting in a tight circle, passing the naked foot from hand to hand in morbid fascination, I still couldn't get over how heavy it felt.

"He didn't cut his toenails!" said Drelaud, handing the foot back to me. "He's got long toenails!"

"He wasn't wearing any socks either," said Nigel.

"Dirty bloody German, that's why!" said Freddie, standing off to one side. Freddie never missed an opportunity to tell everyone how much he hated the Germans – all Germans – and for some reason wanted everyone to know it.

"They found the other pilot over there," said Brian Harrison, "in the next field."

"Alive?" asked Nigel.

"No." said Brian. "My dad said he left it late to jump and his parachute didn't open properly."

Thinking about what Brian had just said, I set the foot down on the grass besides us. Suddenly, before anyone could do anything, Barney, the Harrison's Labrador dog, snatched up the foot and, clamping it firmly in its mouth, ran off with it!

"I wonder if the rest of him is in heaven." I muttered aloud while again picking up the empty boot.

"Who bloody cares!" said Freddie. "I hope the bugger's in hell!"

"That's not right to say." I said.

"Why?" demanded Freddie? "He was a bloody Jerry – right."

"Yes, but," I began.

"So?" he pressed.

"I ... I don't know," I said, unable to explain what I meant to anyone – least of all Freddie.

Meanwhile, after snatching up the dead pilot's foot, Brian Harrison's dog carried it all the way back to their house, where much to the shock and distress of Brian's mother, the animal had deposited its morbid trophy in the middle of their kitchen floor – something for which Brian's mother would forever hold me responsible!

~   ~   ~

12   Wooden clogs and jellied brawn

In May 1944 Allied attacks in the Channel became more frequent and supplies getting through from France to the Island were becoming extremely few and far between, causing critical shortages and an increase in the amount of concern by both the German and local civil authorities. One morning during a sunny weekend, the big Jerry anti-aircraft guns situated beyond the ridge to the rear of the house suddenly opened up on an American B-25 bomber that was flying south over the Island on its way towards St Malo. I ran up to my parents' bedroom and got there just in time to see the B-25 unload a couple of bombs on the German defense battery down at Platt Rocque Point harbour, causing one of the biggest, earth shaking explosions imaginable.

"Wow! That will give the Jerries something to think about," I thought.

Unfortunately, the bombs missed their intended target without doing very much damage, but it was extremely exciting to see and did much to breathe a little hope into the hearts of everyone praying for an end to the war. However, more frighteningly, it also brought home the fact, especially to my mother, that if ever the Allies were to invade the Island, the little air raid shelter at the back of our rear garden would not be enough to protect us when all hell could be let loose!

The following Monday when I rode to school after the B-25 incident at Platt Rocque, I noticed that the Jerries were running around all over the place on the golf course and were engaged in some kind of light manoeuvres. They had also set up a heavy machine gun just inside the Inner Road entrance to the course just across the road from where Elizabeth Colley lived. The whole situation appeared no different to the way it did when we were playing soldiers in the front woods, aiming and firing our wooden rifles at each other – the only difference being, besides the fact we were kids and they were "for real" soldiers, the Jerries had real guns and were shooting live, albeit blank, ammunition.

This of course meant a trip down to the golf course as soon we got out of school to look for any discarded cartridge cases or the pink wooden blank bullet heads that the Jerries used during their exercises. I managed to find half a dozen empty cartridge cases; four pink wooden bullets and one live blank round before anyone else, providing me with some real swapping power.

*   *   *

One morning, Drelaud and Titch arrived at school wearing some locally- made, wooden-soled, tin-tipped clogs. These were the local communities' answer to the fact that, apart from second-hand bartered footwear, there were no longer any new shoes available. Parents either bartered or exchanged hand-me-down shoes for their growing children if they could find any, or they took the option of wooden-soled clogs. As far as we kids were concerned, clogs, in terms of style, were the cat's whiskers – absolutely the thing to be wearing.

The soles were fashioned out of wood, with the uppers formed out of scrap leather or, in some cases, out of heavy painted canvas. Each pair had a tin strip protector tacked on the heel and toe along with a few hobnails on the bottom of the soles; they made a wonderful noise and I just had to have a pair! But my mother hated them, saying that they reminded her too much of horse manure and the wooden straw-lined sabots worn on the farms, and were not the sort of thing I should be wearing to school or church on Sundays. Yet on the other hand, she didn't mind the fact that I ran barefoot during the summer holidays in order to save what shoe leather still remained on the soles of my last pair of soon to be outgrown shoes.

On Wednesday mornings my grandfather, while on his way into town to sit in the States Assembly, would call by the house to deliver some fresh goat's milk for my little sister Diana. My grandmother believed that goat's milk offered greater health benefits than ordinary cow's milk and that it would be far better for Diana's health in the end.

Grumpa, as a member of the Superior Council and generally in the forefront of what was going on within the wartime administration of the

Occupation documents signed by my grandfather

Island, would always call in at our house on his way into town in order to reassure my mother that the war wouldn't last forever. Whenever I was at home on such occasions, he would always make a point of telling us both that regardless of how difficult things might become, we were going to win the war.

Sometimes he would sit and discuss with her some of the latest war news and rumours that were making their way around the Island, or how difficult it was becoming for him and the Council in their continued struggle with the Germans over food rationing, and the allocation of the ever-decreasing amount of fuel supplies.

"See if you can find and get hold of one or two extra candles," he cautiously suggested to my mother. "We're running short of coal – shipments aren't getting through. We may have to cut the electricity and gas supply by the end of this summer."

"God! What next?" said my mother in exasperation. "Right now I'm trying to find Geoffrey some second-hand shoes for school next term. He's either worn through or grown out of everything he has."

"Really!" said my grandfather, "We can't have that now, can we?" Whereupon, he promptly took his wallet out from his breast pocket and produced a "Blue Hitler", a twenty mark Reich note.

"Take this," he said, handing the blue Reich note to my mother. "Get him some of those fancy clogs while they still last – all the kids seem to like them!"

~   ~   ~

Empty shop windows offering Nazi propaganda

Living with the enemy on King Street, St Helier

As food rationing increased and shortages continued to build, the civil authorities provided lunches for school children. Each day at Prep, we would break for lunch and march down to a public dining room and kitchen that was located near the corner of St Saviour's Road and La Motte Street in St Helier. In the course of wartime events, this would not be anything worthy of recording, but on our very first visit to the public facility I experienced one of the most unappetizing meals of my life! Decades later I can still recall the first awful taste of what was dished up as being "jellied brawn" – some awful concoction made from pigs' trotters and who knows what.

Miss Fraser, the head cook, a grumpy, frumpy middle-aged woman in charge, stood in front of her wood-fired stoves from where she could survey the luncheon room with an eagle eye for anyone who might remotely object to her cooking, or even dare question what might be on offer for lunch. One of the kids sitting at our table bent forward to smell the strange fare placed on his plate.

"You don't need to smell it – you fussy brat!" she screamed. "It's good for you! Eat it!"

From then on, at some point along the way while on the walk down from school to the public dining room, the discussion as to whether or not we were going to have to eat any more of that bloody brawn stuff again never failed to surface. As far as I'm able to recall, whatever may or may not have been served up to us for lunch from that time on must have been a lot more palatable, because the jellied brawn never appeared on the menu again. Probably because most of the jellied brawn served on that first fateful day had found its way onto the floor under the long table and been kicked towards someone else's seat.

~   ~   ~

Somehow, Drelaud had managed to get hold of a German bayonet, and to avoid his father catching him, he had to keep it hidden under some books in his school satchel. It was a real beauty; complete with scabbard and belt holster. He told me that he had swapped it with Brian Le Boutillier for his brass telescope, a silver cigarette lighter and three of his best Jerry badges.

"I went and swapped him my silver wired officer's breast eagle," he explained somewhat regretfully.

"Where did Boutie get it?" I asked.

"From some Jerry he knows," he said. "Swapped it with him for some baccie!"

"Baccie?" I questioned.

"Yes, baccie – tobacco," he said. "Jerries will give anything for baccie – if you can get some."

Needless to say, before our conversation had come to an end, I have to somewhat shamefully admit that I had already begun to stealthily entertain the possibilities of making a connection between Fritz, the guard, my father's

13 A bayonet and the live bullet

I arranged to meet Drelaud at the dark end of the cloakroom before the morning bell rang for school, where we would swap his Jerry bayonet for my ammunition collection and three of my best Jerry badges – the Infantry Assault Badge that I got from Fritz, a Luftwaffe anti-aircraft badge and *schnellboot* badge. But after having arrived a little later than usual I was met instead by Miss Painter, who told me to hang my cap and coat up and get on up to the classroom. Not wanting to open my satchel to take out my homework in front of her, I decided to hold on to it and hurried off to the main hall where, at the bottom of the stairs, I found Drelaud, Titch and Bob with a bunch of other kids, all about to make their way up to the various classrooms. The Head Prefect, a real teacher's pet named Stevens, was standing outside Miss Cassimir's study getting ready to ring the school bell and announce the start of morning classes. As I turned and mounted the stairs, Drelaud grabbed my arm.

"Did you bring it?" he asked. "The stuff?"

"Yes." I said. "Did you?"

"Yes. It's in my satchel," he replied, as we began our way up the stairs. "Let me see," said Drelaud, grabbing for my satchel.

"No, not now," I said, pulling the satchel back until it slipped from my grasp and fell, allowing about a hundred empty cartridge cases, which also included at least a dozen and a half live rounds of German rifle ammunition, to spill down onto the marble tiled floor outside Miss Cassimir's study! A mad rush ensued, with everyone helping to pick up the fallen items and get them back into my satchel before anyone came along and wanted to know what we were up to.

"What's going on here?" cried Miss Cassimir, who couldn't believe her eyes when she saw the cartridges noisily rolling around all over the floor.

"Who's responsible for this?" she demanded.

"Norman," said Stevens, putting the hand-bell down. "I think the bullets are his," he continued, picking up a live round and handing it to Miss Cassimir.

"My God! Is this real?" she asked. "Is it live?"

"Oh yes Miss," he gleefully replied. "See there," he continued, proudly pointing to the base of the live round, "the cap hasn't been fired – see, it's still smooth."

Of course, after a severe lecture on the dangers of such behaviour and what could happen if the Germans ever caught any of us with live ammunition, I was sent to the back storeroom where, after having had all my "stuff" confiscated, a furious Miss Painter dished out six of her best whacks! Later in the morning, during class break, I vented my frustration on Drelaud and got into a right punch-up with him over the bayonet and what had happened to all my stuff. However, knowing that he didn't want to get caught with the bayonet by his father, I eventually secured the bayonet on the understanding that he would get all the badges and empty cartridges back at the end of term when all of our confiscated items, except for the live rounds, were to be duly returned.

During those wartime days at Prep, Michael Drelaud was the only kid that I would ever get into a full fight with on a regular basis. The first time, old Reggie Nicolle, our gym teacher, put boxing gloves on us in the playground. While Reggie was lacing me up, Drelaud came up behind me and let go with a sledgehammer swing that caught me in the side of the head, and then ran off. Old Reggie brought him back by the scruff of the neck and then matched us up in the ring where I proved to be the better boxer, but not necessarily the better street scrapper.

While we had been schoolmates ever since our early days at Mandalay, regularly played with each other and mostly got into trouble together, my friendship with Drelaud was never anything like as close as it was with Nigel, Elizabeth or Titch – or any of the other kids. I was always acutely aware that whenever I chose to muck about with Drelaud, no matter how much fun we might have together, we would always inevitability end up in some kind of trouble – a situation that maintained itself all the way through Prep, right up until a couple of years after the war when most of us left to enter Victoria College.

One Saturday morning as Drelaud, Titch, Nigel and I were about to turn for the pathway leading into the front wood, we noticed that there appeared to be no guard on duty at the bottom of the long driveway leading down from the two large houses where the Jerries were billeted. Drelaud suggested that it might be fun to run over to the sentry's phone-box, wind it up and shout, "Hitler is a *schweinhund*" and any other Jerry swearwords we could think of into the receiver and then do a bunk for the woods. As we gathered around the field phone-box and got ready to open it, Nigel and Titch suddenly looked up and noticed Fritz leaning against a section of wall further up the driveway.

It was a place where he could quietly study English with the aid of his little red dictionary or where he could gaze out across Callec's sloping field and the landscape below towards the twinkling sea.

"*Achtung!*" he said sternly, obviously aware that we were up to no good.

"*Das ist nicht gut!*" he continued shaking his head and wagging a finger. Then, putting his little dictionary away, Fritz strolled down the driveway towards us. Strangely, for some reason, we just stood there rather than doing a normal fast bunk.

"*Ah, Jeffie mein freund,*" he said, approaching us with a smile, "How you are today, *gut ja?*"

"Good thank you, *danke* Fritz," I replied.

"You know him?" asked Drelaud.

"Yes," I replied. "He's all right. He's nice."

"He's the one who gave him that good badge," said Nigel.

I really couldn't tell how old Fritz was. Obviously to someone of my age at the time he appeared to me as being a mature looking man who may have been somewhere in his middle to late thirties. I felt sure that he was a bit younger than my father was. He wore his forage cap slightly cocked and I noticed that he had a thin sprinkling of grey hairs and that he generally spoke with a soft and somewhat kindly voice. He didn't shout or speak harshly like many of the other Jerries seemed to do. On earlier occasions, he had shown me a snapshot of his wife and a picture of his baby son who lived somewhere far away in Germany.

Following our round of first name introductions, Fritz looked about and, after making sure that no one in charge unexpectedly came by, he took off his forage cap and allowed both Drelaud and Titch to try it on – a much desired souvenir item that any of us would have willingly given our back teeth for. I had yet to mention anything to Fritz, or anyone else for that matter, about the possibility of swapping some tobacco leaves for souvenirs. The leaves growing in our back garden that I hoped to be able to pick without getting caught would not be ready until sometime in late July, and would have to be dried before I could even think of any serious swapping business.

After looking about to make sure no one was coming, Fritz surprised us by unslinging his rifle, opening the bolt and then sliding it back and forth. He unloaded five rounds of live ammunition. Holding on to the live rounds, Fritz then allowed each one of us to actually hold and aim his rifle. After handing the rifle back to Fritz, we watched as he slowly showed us how to reload each round back into the magazine.

It was not until Fritz slowly slid the last round of live ammunition into the breach of his rifle and closed the bolt that a stark shock of frightening reality hit me. I suddenly became acutely aware that that very bullet might one day kill one of our own British soldiers or perhaps even someone caught out after curfew. Something, right there and then within the pit of my stomach told me that if ever ordered to aim at anyone and pull the trigger, that's exactly what Fritz would have to do!

Later that night as I lay in bed turning over the day's events in my mind, the drone of an approaching aircraft brought the heavy anti-aircraft guns into action. Normally I would have jumped out of bed and opened the corner of the blackout to look out and see the searchlights scanning across the night sky – half hoping they might for a moment lock onto a British or an American bomber. Instead, I just lay in my bed and wondered when the war would end as Grumpa promised and what life would really be like when it was all over. There would be no need for blackout blinds. We'd have sweets, real chocolates, ice-cream, oranges and bananas – things I knew about and had seen pictures of, though I couldn't imagine what they tasted like. Grumpa could have a big fat goose for Christmas and carve roast beef for Sunday lunch instead of the occasional stringy rabbit. My dad could drive his car again and play golf with some lovely new shiny white golf balls. Elizabeth Colley's father would return from England to hug and kiss her again. Peter Cardnell and his mum would come home from Germany and we would all be able to listen to the BBC news on a proper wireless set. My mother could have a cup of real English tea, buy a dress for herself and find some comfortable shoes. We would have real pump-up rubber tyres on our bikes instead of old hosepipe, and be able to go on the beach to play and swim whenever we wanted to. There would be no more Germans, barbed wire and mines. Fritz could go home to his wife and baby instead of worrying about having to go and fight on the Russian Front.

"Oh, what if?" I thought, "What if, what if, and what if …?"

~   ~   ~

14 Sugar beet cubes, cider and Green Island

Mr Mac's magic joint – where both ends of the hosepipe that was serving as my front tyre met – had somehow flattened out. This meant that I had to ride with a recurring bump, bump, bump, that, besides being uncomfortable and somewhat embarrassing, was also driving me batty. As a result, one day after school, I decided to head down to the canning factory and ask Mr Mac if he could fix it for me. Titch, Drelaud and Graham Talbot, a classmate whom we all knew as Tally, elected to come along with me. I had told them about the special dried sugar beet cubes that Paul Boleat, the assistant manager, had been developing and experimenting with in the factory's laboratory, and they all wanted to sample one of the lovely sweet crunchy crouton-sized cubes.

After arriving at the factory we headed for the boiler room in search of Mr Mac, and were told by one of the stokers that he was in the machine room, where we eventually found him busy threading a piece of galvanized pipe. I explained my problem to the old Scot, who took my bike and said he would fix it as soon as he had finished with what he was doing.

Paul Boleat measured out a small handful of his little experimental crispy sugar beet cubes to each of us and after thanking him, we hurried off to the air raid shelter in the garden roundabout where we sat and ate them one by one, much to everyone's satisfaction. The factory was one of the best places in the whole world for a kid to muck about in – there was no end of places to explore, of things to see and touch. The upper can lofts were always fun. We could build a camp out of the empty cardboard boxes that had once contained new cans, or look down on the production line and see the women filling the jars with black sugar beet syrup. In the factory's main warehouse, we played in my father's car, which still lay hidden under a tarpaulin behind a wall of crated cans. Later, while climbing about over a stack of large burlap sacks Tally, seeing a hole in one of the sacks, stuck his finger into what appeared to me to be nothing more than coarse salt, but was instead, as it turned out, real sugar! The finger-sized hole in the sack soon grew to fist size, provoking one of the best all time sugar rushes in the history of the Occupation.

Because the sugar had been part of the factory's inventory before the war, it had not been subject to any mandatory requisition by either civil or German authorities. Years later, I asked my father about the sugar and why he had kept it hidden away during a time when so many people were going hungry.

"Because no matter what we would have done with it, son," he began to explain to me, "it would have ended up on the black market – all of it! Even if we had given it to the hospital or the civil government to be shared and rationed," he continued, "it would have disappeared before anyone knew it. In those days, sugar could fetch sixty bob (sixty shillings/three pounds) or more a pound! And because we didn't have enough to improve the welfare of the overall civilian population, it was better to let it rest quietly where it was."

Paul Boleat's delicious crispy sugar beet cubes definitely paled in comparative sweetness to that which Tally had discovered in the burlap sacks. So Drelaud, feeling very thirsty after having devoured so much sugar, suggested we head back to the air raid shelter and try some of Uncle Edward's cider. At first we were unable to find a corkscrew with which to open one of the bottles, and that was because there was none. Instead, as we soon discovered, a siphon stick with a small tap on its top had to be used due to the pressure that would build up in the bottles as the cider aged. Once we got the siphon inserted, great fun erupted. Turning the little tap on, we were able to squirt the cider from across the other side of the shelter and aim it into each other's mouths – getting a bit of a bath in the process!

Fortunately, before things got completely out of hand, Mr Mac appeared in the shelter doorway to say that he had fixed the tyres on my bike.

"You'd better give me that," he said, pointing to the empty bottle. "And go and wash, because if your daddy ever finds out what you've been up to in here, he'll tan all of your hides!"

In early May, the weather turned warm and Major Heider, the *Platzkommandant*, allowed some of the southern beaches to be opened up to the civilian population and German troops alike. He allowed this mainly because the beaches from Havre des Pas eastwards to Platt Rocque Point (Le Rocque) were bordered by a dense wall of natural coastal reefs which would in all probability discourage any form of Allied seaborne invasion.

Despite all the wartime miseries being suffered both at home and abroad, 1944 in Jersey might well be remembered by some of us for the lovely long, hot sunny summer days when we were able to enjoy playing and swimming on the beach.

Major Heider's summer gesture may well have been the result of efforts by

Baron von Aufsess, the Chief Administrator, who liked both to swim and to gallop Froni, a frisky white mare, bareback across the wide beach down at La Mare. Wearing nothing but his swimming trunks, the Baron would pull up and randomly pick up a couple of younger children and then ride them out into the surf for a splashing frolic – much to the envy of those of us left to stand and watch.

Green Island.
Bottom left: Le Croc Point, four-barrelled 20mm Vierling anti-aircraft gun emplacement

Most of the time we went down to Green Island slipway. This was a popular bay with a small grassy Island sitting just off the shore that was accessible on foot at low tide. My great auntie Nan (Grumpa's sister) lived in a dormer cottage with a lovely garden that ran down to the sea wall at the west end of the bay next to Le Croc Point. There the Jerries had set up a fortified four barreled 20mm Vierling anti-aircraft gun emplacement with a commanding sweep across the bay towards Le Nez Point at the east end where the heavy coastal gun at Rocque Berg sat menacingly looking out to sea. We played on the beach below the barbed wire defences and swam in the early morning or late afternoon high tide that would allow us to dive off the end of the jetty, and when the tide was out during the day, we would cross over to Green Island itself and swim in the abandoned breeder.[11]

Every so often, a platoon of Jerries under the command of an officer or a

---

11 *A deep artificial tide pool created between the rocks by installing a granite wall at each end — used to keep and breed lobster and crab.*

senior NCO (non-commissioned officer) would arrive at Green Island slipway with a heavy anti-tank gun in tow behind a lorry. They would then close the beach and clear everyone off it before positioning the gun above the sea wall near the top of the slipway.

In the meantime, we would all gather around to observe from a short distance. Usually the officer in charge would have the platoon line up in rank and wait before taking individual turns at firing off a dozen or so rounds of large calibre ammunition, all aimed at some of the prominent rock formations out to sea, and then at some of the rocks that were closer to the surrounding beach.

"Why do they always line up in rank with the tallest soldier in front and the smallest one at the back?" asked Titch.

"I don't know," I answered, obviously trying to be somewhat sensitive to the fact that Titch was the smallest amongst us.

"They do it that way so when they attack, the littler soldier at the back can hide behind the bigger one in front," explained Nigel.

"But if the smaller soldier was in front, then the bigger soldier behind could shoot over the top of the littler soldier – wouldn't that be better?" reasoned Titch. This made sense to me.

"No." replied Bob from behind his floppy forelock of sandy-blond hair. "The way they do it allows the taller soldier in front to get shot first, then the little one at the back can step forward and fire in his place!"

No matter what the situation, one could always rely on Bob to provide a perfect if not reasonable explanation for anything and everything, even if he had no idea what he was talking about.[12]

When it was all over and the Jerries had packed up and driven off, we would hurry back down onto the beach and head out towards the targeted rocks to search for and collect bits and pieces of shrapnel before the tide came in.

Such was the way in which little boys filled their days during that summer of 1944, and all the way until the end of the Occupation.

~   ~   ~

---

12 *A talent Bob would combine in later years with an air of pure charm that could steal the whiskers off the most feline of felines. After the war, he was the first among us to style his hair in an American crew cut, but resolutely refused to accept it as such. "No, what I have is not American!" he would say with an air of adopted sophistication recently acquired while on a trip to France. "What I have is a 'Le Brosse'," he would say, "It's a French cut – nothing American about it at all!"*

15 The man from Czechoslovakia

One morning, as I was walking home after a high tide swim down at Green Island, I stopped to watch a gang of forced labourers who were working on the railway lines where they crossed Samarés Lane by the old abandoned railway station. A very bored-looking Jerry guard leaned against the wall, while an OT supervisor, a short miserly looking individual wearing a khaki uniform with a red and black Nazi armband shouted orders at the bedraggled workers. As I stood there, a German van turned off the Inner Road and drove down and parked near us. It had brought lunch for the workers. The OT supervisor blew a whistle and yelled at everyone to break for lunch. The workers hungrily gathered and lined up at the back of the van where they were handed a tin plate, a spoon and a ladle helping of boiled cabbage and beans with half a slice of bread. Each man took his portion and then looked for some quiet area to sit and rest as much as a place to eat. One of the workers, a tall friendly looking man with sparkling eyes and a strong square jaw, someone I assumed to have come from somewhere in Eastern Europe or Russia, sat down on the nearby kerb with his plate and spoon for what in all probability would be his one and only meal of the day. Looking up at me, he smiled, gesturing, inviting me to share part of his lunch with him. Knowing full well how poorly they were being fed, I thanked him and, declining his offer, decided to sit down beside him on the kerb outside the long-ago boarded up station news-stand where, incongruously, faded flaking adverts for chocolates, ice-cream and cigarettes still clung to the front wall.

"Ruski?" I asked. For some reason my imagination had been busied with questions concerning the Russian prisoners and workers. From all the rumours and gossip one heard, Russian soldiers had and were giving the Jerries a real tough fight.

"No Ruski. Me Czech – Czech-Slovakia."

"Oh." I said.

"You English yes?" he asked.

"British," I answered. "I'm British."

"Ah yes!" he said. "Grand Britain, yes?"

Breaking a piece off his half slice of bread, he offered it to me. Nodding my head, I declined.

"No. No." he insisted. "You eat – goot for me you eat."

Much to his delight, I took the little piece of bread and ate it.

"Goot!" he said, nodding with great satisfaction before adding, "Goot, we eat together."

Although the lunch break was short, we were able to discuss a number of subjects through his broken English, such as an exchange of names, though sadly today I cannot remember his. He asked how old I was, where I lived and whether or not the sea was warm enough for a swim.

As we sat there together, I noticed another worker, a younger man with a shaved head, who seemed to be walking about quite happily, though for the life of me when considering his situation, I could not imagine how he could seem to be cheerful about anything. He was wearing nothing more than a pair of soiled trousers held together by a piece of thin rope knotted around his waist, while for shoes all this poor fellow had on the soles of his feet was a thick layer of black tar mixed with some fine gravel.

The Nazi OT supervisor blew his whistle, ending the lunch break. Bidding me goodbye, my new friend got up and, after handing in his plate and spoon to the attendant at the van, followed the others back to work on the gravel railway bed. On the way, he turned and winked back at me. I half lifted my hand and waved with a wiggle of my fingers.

I waited for the Jerry van to drive off and head back the way it had come before heading off myself, when suddenly, while my Czech friend was helping to lift a large box down from a flatbed bogie and without any warning, the nasty Nazi Organisation Todt supervisor grabbed him and, pulling him back by the scruff of his shirt collar, began to beat and whip the poor man with a heavy cane until he fell to the ground. He was brutally kicked and beaten until he broke and cried like a child – no one daring to look up or stop work in order to help him. For a moment I stood paralysed and unable to move or say anything – desperately wanting someone to help my poor friend. The Jerry guard, who had been leaning against the wall, came to life, cocked his rifle in a warning gesture to the forced labourers, making it clear what he would do should anyone dare question the OT's action. Immediately I thought of Fritz and of the live bullet that he had so smoothly slid into the breech of his own rifle. I had never before seen or experienced such brutality, let alone seen a grown man cry. When the beating was over and the Jerry guard had lowered his rifle, it was the young man with the tarred feet who dared to move and assist my fallen friend. Bravely, he lifted the broken man back onto his feet and, putting an arm around him, steadied him for a moment until the OT Supervisor began yelling at them to get back to work.

Unable to stand there and look any more and feeling too ashamed to even make eye contact with my beaten friend, I turned and ran up the lane as fast as I could, my mind screaming out in anger – I wanted to kill that rotten little Nazi swine of an OT supervisor, but there was absolutely nothing I could do.

Upon reaching the top of the lane I stopped and turned, wanting to scream but unable to so much as open my mouth. Instead, I blindly ran for the rabbit patch in the front wood, where, desperately upset and angry with myself, I sat in the sun at the base of one of the taller trees.

From where I sat I gazed out across the meadow below the low wall and watched the big Jersey bull slowly lick his ringed nostrils one at a time. All that immense power locked within its powerful body just standing there – idly doing nothing! Much in the way all the forced workers and I had stood while the little Nazi swine had brutally beaten all traces of human dignity from my new friend.

"*Schweinhund!*" I screamed at the bull. "You bloody *schweinhund!* Why didn't you do something?"

I got up and went over to the top of the low wall where I continued swearing at the bull, screaming out every profanity I could find in my young vocabulary of multilingual obscenities. Ignoring me, the bull just stood there, bearing the ring of restraint through his nose as one would when facing a loaded rifle in the hands of the Jerry guard.

"Who are you shouting at?"

I recognized Elizabeth Colley's voice from behind me and turning, saw that she was making her way down through the flowering shrubs towards me.

"No one," I replied. "I was shouting at the bloody bull."

"Why?" she asked, "What's it done?"

"Nothing." I replied. "It just stands there and does nothing."

"Well so would you," she said, arriving on the wall beside me, "especially if you had a ring through your nose and were tied to a rope like that."

"No I wouldn't." I said. "I'd do something."

"What?" she asked.

"I don't know," I replied, "but something."

"My mum says every man should have a ring through his nose." she said with a slight chuckle.

"Why?" I asked.

"I don't know," she replied. "It's meant to be some sort of grown-up joke – have you been crying?" she asked.

"No." I replied, turning toward the tree where I had left my towel and bathing trunks.

"Your eyes are all red," she continued.

"It's the salt – from swimming this morning." I explained, picking up the towel and wiping my face. "Anyway, I have to go."

"Go where?" she asked.

"I have to go over to Uncle Edward's and pick up some spuds and veggies for my mum." I replied.

"I'll go with you if you like," she said suggestively, "and we can play 'doctors and nurses' or 'mothers and fathers' up in the hay loft – one or the other if we have time?"

Playing "doctors and nurses" meant pretending to be sick and in desperate need of an operation. Ultimately, it was about examining each other, getting a peek at each other's bare bum, and wondering at the differences in our plumbing arrangements.

"Fathers and mothers" had the same ends, in a manner of speaking. She would have me playing the father while she in turn would play both her mother and herself.

"Our daughter Elizabeth has been very naughty," she would declare. "And I want you to give her a good thrashing on her bare bottom!"

Such were the ways in which we as children unravelled the wonders and mysteries of it all, while our parents struggled to keep us alive amid the ever-increasing deprivations of the German Occupation.

To this day – almost seventy years later – I can still hear the screams of that poor prisoner when brutally beaten by the OT supervisor. The memory still brings up deep emotions and a figurative tear to my eye, when I think back on the innocence of us as kids going about the natural business of growing up amid the most unnatural atmosphere of wartime.

~   ~   ~

16   D-Day 1944 and Hamptonne on a Sunday

When the news about the Allied landing in Normandy spread throughout the Channel Islands, great hopes were raised for a speedy delivery from the German Occupation. Everyone was hungry, not just for food, but for the smallest scraps of BBC news that could be garnered through hidden crystal sets and then spread throughout the various workplaces.

In anticipation of an impending Allied attack, either by air or an invasion storming our beaches, the Germans put their garrisons on high alert. On our way to school we saw detachments of Jerry troops, all wearing helmets instead of their usual soft forage caps, setting up machine-gun nests at various points along the way. When riding by I had even noticed that Fritz was wearing a helmet instead of his usual cap, which disturbingly made him look unfamiliarly different from the man I'd come to know. Other times, while studying English with his little red dictionary, and when no officer was likely to be coming or going, he would set his helmet down on the wall beside him, explaining that it became tryingly heavy on his neck when having to keep it on all day. Naturally, when learning this, my first thoughts went right to the fact that if he wasn't going to be wearing his forage cap while on duty, perhaps he might be open to swapping it for some dried tobacco leaves.

I liked Fritz. However, due to the horrible incident between the Nazi OT swine and my Czech worker friend, I steered clear of him for a while and allowed some of the feelings that were going on inside me to settle down. As kids we had often to be reminded that we were at war, and that "there was no such thing as a good German – only a dead German." But for me holding such a position when it came to the likes of Fritz the guard was becoming a little difficult, and very confusing to say the least.

~   ~   ~

During one of our Sunday afternoon tea gatherings around the table in the main dining room at Hamptonne, my grandfather broached the subject of his concerns about the coming days to the family. The German response to the Allied landings in Normandy, he explained, appeared to be divided, and their full intentions weren't yet being made clear.

"What do you mean divided?" asked my father.

"Well, if St Malo falls to the Allies and we get cut off from all supplies, hardliners like Hüffmeier will want to hold out and fight to the last man – no matter what the cost," he cautiously explained, "while von Schmettow and von Aufsess, being more reasonable, might allow an approach to the International Red Cross so that we could acquire some civilian relief."

"Oh God, that would be nice!" said my mother. "When might that be?"

"No idea," replied my grandfather, "but we've suggested this to Coutanche, the Bailiff, and he's going to quietly approach them on the idea before any formal requests are made."

"Why quietly, and why not go ahead now, formally, before it's too late?" asked Uncle Edward, getting up from the table to retrieve his tobacco pouch and pipe from the mantelpiece.

"Well," said my grandfather, "until St Malo, which is to the south of us, falls or we get totally cut off, it's up to the German Military Governor in France. He's the one who's still in charge and rumour has it that he wants everyone who is not essential or actively involved in producing food to be evacuated!"

"Evacuated!" exclaimed my mother. "Where?"

"We don't know," answered my grandfather, "it's just a rumour."

"Perhaps they'll allow neutral ships to come in and evacuate everyone," suggested Uncle Edward in an attempt to ease the tension around the dining room table.

"What is certain is this," continued my grandfather, "If we become cut off from France without any supplies or relief getting into the Island, then we are going to end up contending with the German garrison for our survival!"

"Contending, Jim?" asked Auntie Nan, shifting uncomfortably in her chair. "What exactly are you saying?"

"The Germans will be forced into drawing upon all of our civilian food reserves," he explained flatly.

"He means the rotten blighters will start requisitioning everything," said Uncle Edward, after exchanging tobacco pouches with my father and filling his pipe – thereby sampling each other's home-grown Occupation efforts.

"It may well come down to that," said my grandfather.

"But they can't ..." began my mother.

"By declaring such action a military necessity," said my grandfather, "they can do almost anything they want."

"This is getting a little too depressing for me," said my grandmother, getting up from her chair with a sigh. "God only knows where it'll all end."

*　　*　　*

Uncle Edward, 1936

Hamptonne

After tea, I wandered outside towards the stables where I felt a visit to Maurice and Charlie might liven things up. Old Pat and her puppy Scamp, Uncle

Edward's two wire-haired terriers, followed me through the garden.

I found the two old grizzled farmhands sitting in the afternoon sun outside the cow stable on a battered bench with their backs absorbing the warmth from the granite wall. Each was nursing a tankard of cider that had been pressed from the apples in the orchard. They were simple souls, and would perhaps be called "challenged" today.

Old Maurice, as the famous Jersey artist Edmund Blampied might have pictured him in the 1926 London Studio Publication

Both Old Maurice and Charlie had worked for Uncle Edward at Hamptonne for many years. They were both good-natured and one thing was for sure – Maurice, the older of the two, could swear in both English and Jersey-French better than anyone I knew or had ever heard.

"But I farts best in Breton French me!" he would declare with a triumphal air in his broad anglicised Jersey patois.

Charlie, on the other hand, was far more mentally challenged than his older brother. Somewhere in his mid-forties, he was a truly simple weathered soul who spoke and understood nothing but Jersey-French. In those days, Charlie and others like him held a productive place within the farming community, and the community saw to it that they were taken care of; people such as Uncle Edward found them a place. Charlie's main job at Hamptonne was taking the cows to and from pasture and mucking out the stables. It was a job he faithfully discharged while rarely uttering a word or comment from morning to night.

Most of the time he would plod along in his wooden sabots, which he stuffed with straw and garlic, nodding or chuckling in agreement with whatever it was that Old Maurice had to say. Though it must be said that as funny and entertaining as Old Maurice could be, except for when talking about low tide fishing in the gullies below Le Hocq *cauchie*[13] (a subject and activity in which he was considered an expert) Maurice didn't always make a lot of sense in what he said either – not for me anyway.

"If you pour a bucket of petrol onto a fire you," he declared one day with a faint air of imagined authority, "it will just douse her out you ay – it won't burn like you think you – *Ce verre*.[14] But," he continued, "If you throw a match in a can of petrol you, then, *mon Dou*[15], she will explode like a Jerry fart!"

I asked Old Maurice how the strawberries were coming along.

"If the birds or the Jerries don't get them first," he said, "we might 'ave a good crop us this year ay. There's already a couple of ripe ones out there for you ay."

"Why would the Jerries get them?" I asked.

"Ah, them *pourchay*[16] buggers steal from us like gypsies ay," he explained. "The buggers come at night them ay – and blame it on the Russian workers in the mornin' – them poor buggers. But I seen their bloody Jerry boot marks me – on the path an all I have – the *pourchay* buggers!"

"What about the asparagus?" I asked. "Are there any left?"

"Ah yes ay," he replied. "We 'ave us another week or so for them yet."

Charlie downed the last of his cider, burped as if no one was around and then plodded over to the granite water trough, cranked the pump handle up and down and rinsed out his tankard.

"*Wharro*[17] *mon vier*," said Old Maurice, setting his tankard down on the bench beside him, "Marie wants some dry *vraic*[18] for the kitchen fire her ay – so let's you and me get the cart and we'll go down to the *cauchie* an' get some *vraic* for her – an' while we're there we can see us what them Jerry *pourchay* buggers are up to – now the Allies is getting a bit closer to them an all ay?"

~   ~   ~

---

13 *Cauchie – Jèrriais – slipway*
14 *Ce verre – Jèrriais – It's true*
15 *Mon Dou – Jèrriais – My God*
16 *Pourchay – Jèrriais – pig, swine*
17 *Wharro – Jèrriais greeting – 'what ho'*
18 *Vraic – Jèrriais – seaweed*

17 The mascot and a "Jerry bag" in the park

The warm pleasant weather of June 1944 gave promise to the possibility that our summer school holidays might be filled with lovely long hot days on the beach – depending, of course, on whether or not the Jerries would allow them to remain open. In the meantime, rumours of the Allied advance into France did little to alleviate the continued stress our parents suffered against the ever-increasing shortages of food and fuel.

Even at the risk of getting shot, people began violating the late night curfew in order to scrump, scavenge and steal food from both fields and private gardens. As a result, Bottice Callec, like other farmers across the Island, had to string electrified wires through the crops in his field at the back of our house, though with doubtful effect. We all knew that some of the hungry slave workers would understandably sneak out at night in a desperate search for something to eat, but then, as Old Maurice would have said, "so did the bloody Jerries do the same them ay!"

"Especially those," I thought, "like Fritz and the other soldiers who were conveniently billeted in the houses just above Callec's field."

One of the things that caught my attention and the interest of some of my classmates during those early days of summer 1944, was the regular sight of a young fair-haired, blue-eyed Russian boy walking about town fully dressed in a miniature German uniform, complete with insignias, jackboots, belt and bayonet. Aged no more than twelve or thirteen, and standing barely taller than me, he wore a real forage cap cocked to the right of his head – a souvenir the likes of which I desperately wanted to get my hands on. On top of which the very thought of a full military uniform tailored to fit a kid's size, whether German or British, was absolutely intriguing to us – we all wanted to have one.

After being badly wounded and abandoned during the violent turmoil of war on the Eastern Front, this young Slavic-looking boy became the adopted mascot of some frontline German unit, which evacuated him to the Island in order that he could rest and recuperate.

After school, the continued warm weather drew us down to the swimming pool at Havre des Pas in the afternoons. There amongst the sunbathing off-duty Jerries we'd swim and dive, and it was on one such occasion that I looked up from the water to the stands above the diving boards and saw the little Russian mascot, with his badly burnt left arm and hand still bandaged, looking down at us.

It appeared to me as though he wished he could play about with us in the water. After toweling myself down, I went up and sat beside him on the stands. To be truthful, I was probably more interested and fascinated by his real soldier's uniform and how he came to have it, rather than in him personally. I seized the opportunity to examine everything up close for myself.

His forage cap looked the same as the one Fritz wore, but unlike Fritz, he could not speak a single word of English.

Although the mascot took a distant and somewhat guarded

Russian mascot with bandaged war wounds, 1943

Left: Russian mascot, 1945

attitude towards my friendly approach, we were, by means of physical and facial gestures, able to exchange a few pleasantries. Eventually, I discovered that he had never learned how to swim and appeared to suggest that once his wounds had healed, he would like to learn. We continued to sit together in silence until, after a moment or so, he made a series of diving gestures with his uninjured arm – pointing first to the water and then to one of the lower diving boards below – he indicated that he wanted to see me dive off the board into the water.

"Why not?" I thought, "perhaps if I oblige him he might be willing to swap his forage cap for something."

I did my best dive, and then swam back up to the surface as hard as I could so that I would be able to pop waist high out of the water and wave with both arms to the young mascot, but when I emerged, he was gone! He had disappeared, and for what reason, well, who could know?

After what appeared to be a full recovery from his wounds, one could occasionally see the young Russian mascot strutting his jackboots through town. I never had any further exchanges with him, however. Later, and shortly before the fall of St Malo, not having seen him for a while, I thought perhaps he'd been evacuated on one of the last convoys to leave the Channel Islands. It was not until after the war when I saw a picture of him in a local liberations review that I learned what had happened to him. Apparently, our liberating troops had picked him up and deported him along with the rest of the German garrison.

Speaking of that last convoy, my father had sat sadly with a pair of binoculars and watched as it sailed for France, until the last vessel disappeared behind the rocky reef-heads of La Sambue. Besides transporting a number of local civilian prisoners to French prisons and German concentration camps, the convoy was also carrying away his beloved Morris Cowley with the chrome wire wheels. The Germans had finally been able to confiscate the car after someone had spitefully informed the Gestapo of its hidden whereabouts at the factory.

~   ~   ~

Because I often arrived home late after school after having been mucking about with my friends, my mother would occasionally insist that I meet her in Howard Davis Park after school as a punishment. Then, with my sister in her pram, we would return home where I was required to get on with my homework before doing anything else.

On one such occasion as we strolled through the park on our way back home, my mother suddenly pulled up and stopped. I turned to see what she was looking at, and saw a group of Jerry soldiers gathered around a couple of young women who were sitting on a bench. I could also see my mother's face begin to redden with anger.

"What's the matter?" I asked her.

"Nothing," replied my mother curtly.

One of the young women looked up and immediately recognized my mother.

I recognised her as Coleen, the pretty maid who had come to help my mother out for a week or so when our housekeeper Mrs Elliot was home sick and unable to come to work.

The flirting smile on Coleen's face suddenly drained into one of flushed embarrassment.

"Come on, let's go!" said my mother, turning to furiously march off with my sister in the pram.

"That was Coleen," I said, catching up with her.

"I know," said my mother angrily.

"Well?" I began feeling somewhat confused about why she had suddenly become so angry. "She was only talking with those Jerries."

"That's what most 'Jerry bags' do," said my mother sharply.

I rode slowly and balanced my bicycle beside her as we continued on towards home in silence.

I really wanted to talk about Coleen and why my mother was so angry with her for talking to some Jerries in the park. I well understood how much my father hated the Germans; they were after all, the enemy. But I often felt quite uncomfortable when overhearing my mother when it came to the subject of "Jerry bags" or "horizontal collaborators", as she would put it – an expression I didn't quite understand.

It wasn't until later that evening when we had sat down to supper that the real source of her anger was revealed across the table to my father.

"I saw Coleen in the park today!" she declared. "That little Jerry bag!"

My father looked up from his meal, steadying himself for whatever it was that was about to fly his way.

"Coleen?" asked my father. Then remembering: "Oh, her."

"Yes her!" affirmed my mother. "Besides flirting with a bunch of Jerries, she was wearing a skirt that she had obviously made up out of the curtain material she stole from the top shelf of my airing cupboard!"

~   ~   ~

The lovely sunny weather continued into July, allowing us to run barefoot at the weekends, and doing much to entice both Germans and civilians to relax on the designated beaches. Nevertheless, despite the encouraging prospects for a bountiful harvest of summer wheat, it was still a month of ever-increasing anxieties. The ongoing Allied drive into Normandy and its advance towards the ancient, heavily fortified, walled city and port of St Malo, the Island's main source of supplies, was putting the German garrison under ever-increasing pressure. In addition, as my grandfather had warned us while sitting around the dining room table at Hamptonne, the German High Command was now openly considering plans to draw down upon all of our civilian food reserves in preparation for a siege if Berlin were to command them to stand and fight until the last man. For this was what the orders were for all German troops

18 The last harvest

The summer school holidays of 1944 couldn't come fast enough for my friends and me. I was desperate to get back to mucking about in the woods and being able to attend to some of the more important things in a "*Boys Own*"[19] world. Things we had all been required to put aside for the sake of reading, writing, and Miss Painter's endless arithmetic classes. In my case, the ripening tobacco leaves growing in the back garden were now calling out for some serious attention before my father set about harvesting the entire crop in one swoop – because when that was done, it would be nigh on impossible for me to get up into the loft without being caught!

Carefully, and without being seen, I was able to pick about a dozen large leaves from near the bottom of the tall stalks; leaves that had already begun to turn brownish gold in colour. Once I had got them safely up into my bedroom, I climbed up onto the chest of drawers and set about laying the big leaves out to dry on the top of my wardrobe next to my Jerry bayonet, which I had also stored there for safe keeping.

Every so often, when I had worn my parents out and almost driven them round the bend, they would pack me off to Grumpa's house for a couple of weeks. So after school broke up for the summer holidays in early August, it wasn't too long before my mother asked if I would like to go and spend some time with Grumpa, which was just fine by me until we arrived at Anneville Lodge, whereupon my father went and ruined the whole arrangement.

"Do you think you could tutor Geoffrey?" my father asked as we walked into Grandma's kitchen. "He needs a little help with some of his school work."

"Of course," replied my grandmother, "I'd be more than happy to."

"An hour or so in the mornings," suggested my father.

"What a rotten trick," I thought to myself, "I should have stayed at home!"

The quiet beach down at Havre de Fer Arquerondel (known today as Archirondel) below Grumpa's house was also opened up to the public, and every afternoon during the lovely warm summer half a dozen local housewives, including my grandmother, would gather to sit in the sun on the rocks below the barbed wire surrounding the Martello tower. This also gave my grandmother

---

19 *"Boys Own" was a pre-war magazine for boys*

the opportunity to collect a special kind of seaweed from among the rocks that enabled her to make gelatine, while others, including some off-duty German soldiers, collected winkles, limpets or the odd crab for supper. Unfortunately the pickings were usually slim due to the fact that the lower part of the beach, where one really needed to go in order to obtain any kind of reasonable catch when the tide was out, was still fortified with steel tank traps, barbed wire and mines, making it unreachable.

Arquerondel Bay

The summer wheat field, 1940

Nevertheless, Ralph and I were happy to fish the tide pools for cabots[20], catch a few small shrimps with our junior nets and swim together at high tide. For some reason, Ralph never really tried, nor did he ever appear to even want, to learn how to swim. So while I swam, he would just walk along on his hands at the shallow edge of the water with his legs trailing, kick his feet and do no more.

---

20 *Small rockfish*

When the wheat was gathered, bound into sheaves and then stacked in circular tents up and down the field, Ralph and I would play hide-and-seek – hiding from each other by scrambling under one of these many golden tents. We quickly became friends.

Sometime during the early autumn of that year on one of our weekend visits to Anneville Lodge, I unexpectedly overheard a conversation between my grandmother and my parents. I had barely entered the little hallway outside the kitchen, when I heard her tell them about the sudden and tragic details of Ralph's death.

Apparently, while no one was about, Ralph had wandered along the sea wall at high tide near the south end of the bay towards La Crête Point when he slipped and accidentally fell into the water and drowned! When they found him at low tide it was too late. Ralph was dead – and his parents would remain forever heartbroken.

Stunned by the unexpected news, I quietly withdrew and quickly headed for my secret place. As I breathlessly climbed the path through the tall *côtil* bracken and past the flowering rhododendrons, I thought of Peter Cardnell and his mother in Germany – they had gone too. Most of all, I was confused as to why I didn't feel more upset about Ralph than I thought I should have been. Damn it! If only Ralph had learnt to swim! It would be many years later before I could ever allow myself to tearfully grieve for the loss of my dear friend, Ralph.

~   ~   ~

Grumpa tied a little piece of bright red wool onto the end of a short fishing line which had been attached to the railings surrounding the pond down at the end of the front garden, and dropped it into the water. The young eels had arrived after swimming all the way from the Sargasso Sea so that they might grow in the quiet waters flowing through the pond. Once the eels bit down on the red wool their very fine teeth became so entangled that it became near impossible for them to wriggle free. Hopefully, on visiting the pond in the next day or so we would have a catch of some sort that my grandmother could prepare for a tasty lunch or supper. I liked to watch in amazement as she cut the eels up into short pieces after cleaning and preparing them and see the pieces continue to wriggle away in the frying pan!

I followed Grumpa up the garden path towards the front of the lodge and as we passed the waterfall we suddenly saw a German officer casually standing in the garden near the drawing room veranda. I immediately recognised him as the one we'd seen down at La Mare beach giving some of the kids a splashing ride on his horse through the surf and then all the way across the beach and back. He turned and smiled when he saw us approaching.

"You've chosen a lovely day to spend in your garden Jurat, Sir," said von Aufsess, politely addressing my grandfather in perfect English while tipping his cap in a casually unmilitary manner.

"Good afternoon Baron." said my grandfather. "What brings the *Kommandant* to my garden?"

"Well, I would like to say the sheer horticultural beauty that it offers," he replied looking up at the flowering rhododendrons, "but unfortunately, there are one or two little wartime matters that I'd like to discuss with you – off the record that is … if it isn't too much of an imposition."

My grandfather would not invite him into his house; instead he led the Baron up onto the veranda and offered him a seat in one of the white wicker armchairs. Von Aufsess removed his cap and placed it on one of the side tables. I rather liked the look of Baron's cap because it had a somewhat softer look about it, with a casual slouchy style shape moulded into it rather than the rigid Prussian sharp-edged high-peaked caps worn by most of the other senior German officers.

The other thing I noticed about the Baron was the fact that he kept the holstered pistol on his belt well out of the way behind his left arm as though it was something he didn't want to be bothered by.

"This is my grandson," said my grandfather, introducing and making me feel very important. "Geoffrey, this is Colonel Baron von Aufsess."

Von Aufsess immediately reached for his cap and putting it back on, stood up out of his chair and with a broad smile, snapped a smart salute toward me.

"How do you do, Geoffrey," said the Baron.

"You may return the colonel's salute if you like – as a mark of respect for his rank," offered my grandfather, "but until the war is over and won, we do not shake hands with the Germans."

I tried to take in what my grandfather had said, but had to let it pass over me while the somewhat dashing officer's presence and his courteous demeanour felt a little overwhelming for me.

"How do you do Sir," I said, and saluted the smiling Baron as smartly as I was able.

"Thank you," replied the Baron, overlooking my grandfather's admonition to me.

Von Aufsess paused for a moment before taking off his cap again and sitting down to cast his eyes about the garden and up at the flowering rhododendrons in the *côtil*, taking in all the flowerbeds and shrubs and the waterfall.

"If wars could be fought with flowers," said the Baron, "then this poor beleaguered Island could conquer the whole continent."

"Geoffrey!" came a sudden cry from my grandmother that echoed through the *côtil*. "Geoffrey!"

"You'd better go see what you grandmother wants," said my grandfather quietly. "Sounds like she's in the kitchen garden."

"But …" I began, not wanting to leave.

"Say goodbye to the *Kommandant* and run along," said my grandfather. "Don't keep your grandmother waiting."

Von Aufsess turned and smiled while I reluctantly took my leave and trotted off to see what my grandmother wanted.

When I arrived she was standing outside the back door.

"Oh, there you are," she said.

"There's a German officer …" I started to say.

"Yes. Yes. I know," she replied. "Run up and keep the goats quiet," she continued. "We don't want to let him know we have goats in the *côtil*."

"Who?" I asked.

"The German officer silly," answered my grandmother. "If he finds out we have goats he'll send some soldiers to take them away – go quickly. Go!"

When I reached the goats in the *côtil*, they were quietly nibbling away at the grass and whatever else they could find. That morning they had been tethered near one of the two beehives my grandparents kept and after patting and reassuring Nanny and her kid Billy, I sat in the quiet solitude of the *côtil* and listened to the buzz of the busy bees as they came and went to harvest and deliver the precious pollen that provided us with a touch of sweetness amid our wartime scarcities.

After about forty-five minutes or so I heard what sounded to me like the German officer opening and closing the front gate and then the sound of his car driving off. Being eager as I was to find out what the officer had wanted to talk to Grumpa about, I got up and quickly started back down the narrow bracken-lined path towards the house, only to meet Grumpa on his way up. He had a small chip basket in his hand and suggested we look for some mushrooms in the upper field.

"Grumpa?" I asked as we began to climb together through the *côtil*. "The German officer…?"

"Yes. What about him?" asked Grumpa in reply.

"Well," I began, "What did he want?" I asked as we climbed together through the *côtil*.

"Well, the Allies are getting close to capturing St Malo and the Jerries know they're losing the war," he began. "And the Baron is concerned about the Island becoming short of fuel, food shortages and deforestation – and some other things that I can't go into should the Allies cut off our supply lines."

"What's that? The de…forest thing you said?" I asked.

"You mean deforestation?" he asked.

"Yes – what's that mean?" I asked.

"Well in this case, it means cutting down too many trees," he explained. "Like clearing a forest or cutting down all these trees on our *côtil*."

"Why would you want to do that?" I persisted.

"If we have another cold winter like last year, and our coal supplies from France are cut off, then we may have no choice other than to start cutting a lot of trees for fuel."

"Including some of these trees?" I asked looking about the *côtil* and trying to imagine the place without any of its trees.

"It could come to that," said my grandfather. "We just don't know. We'll just have to wait until St Malo falls and then see what happens."

"Will it?" I asked.

"What?" asked my grandfather.

"St Malo? Will it fall?"

"Oh, yes," he replied affirmatively. "Very soon I expect – very soon."

I had already heard the distant booms of the raging battle that was swirling the outskirts of St Malo some thirty miles away as I sat looking out across the bay from my secret place up on the point. The more violent and explosive face of war was now within a short distance of our shores and some people, including the hard-line Jerries, began to worry about what would happen if the Allies decided to invade the Island, while others like my grandfather and the Baron von Aufsess seemed to worry more about the Island being strangled – being cut off and isolated without any lines of supply.

~   ~   ~

19   Leaflets, ovens and hay-boxes

On 18 August, 1944, the ancient walled city of St Malo finally fell to the Americans.   Colonel von Aulock, the German commander ordered to fight to the last man, was taken prisoner.   As far as any future food and fuel supplies were concerned, the Channel Islands were now completely cut off from all their mainland sources.   Any hope of survival was destined to become intensely difficult for everyone.   Shortages in fuel supplies to even maintain public utilities threatened a total breakdown of Island life.

As the distant booms from the mounting siege of St Malo some thirty miles away drifted toward us, relations between the *Feldkommandantur* and the Superior Council became difficult and increasingly strained.   Several adventurous young men had escaped from the local prison, while others secretly prepared to escape across the fourteen-mile stretch of water that lay between the Island and the nearest beach in France.   As a result, Major Heider, the German Military *Platzkommandant*, threatened to close down all the beaches in a reprisal against the civilian population.   Fortunately, the major's anger was subdued and this did not happen.

A large number of evacuated German sailors and soldiers, many of them very badly wounded during the siege of St Malo, suddenly arrived in Jersey. This put an immediate and enormous strain, not only on the scarce food reserves, but also on the very limited stocks of available medical supplies. Surgical procedures were immediately restricted to life-threatening cases. Within a few short months, by mid November of 1944, the situation would see most medical treatments and services nearly coming to a complete standstill.

A few nights after the siege we were all woken up by the sound of big anti-aircraft guns firing on Allied planes that were flying over the Islands and dropping thousands of leaflets printed in both German and English in a vain attempt to get the Germans to consider surrendering.   This they defiantly rejected.

Some of the mixed leaflets contained an overall report on the latest Allied advances into Europe, while others offered general news of their far-flung war efforts, enough to bring everyone up-to-date and correct some of the wildly inaccurate rumours that had been circulating. As the leaflets had been randomly dropped and scattered through the night skies across the Island, many were immediately gathered up before the Germans could confiscate them and as such became popular items that we could swap with each other at school; I managed to acquire quite a fistful.

My father, having read most of the leaflets already circulated around the factory, chose three or four from my collection that he thought might offer the Jerries the most poignant reminder of their now uncertain war situation.

"We have to place them right where they can't miss them," he said. "Right up under old Jerry's nose."

Naturally, my mother was not too happy about the idea of him going out and violating the strict curfew in what she saw as no more than an act of pointless defiance and became quite irritated with him as the evening darkened.

"Why get yourself shot for doing something so damned futile?" she exclaimed. "What on earth do you expect to gain by such a trivial deed?"

"It's the thought and action that counts," countered my father. "As futile and trivial as it may seem to you, believe me, the Jerries won't see it as such." he further asserted.

"That's my whole point – damn it!" replied my mother, as he went out into the night.

After about forty minutes of anxious waiting, we heard my father closing the back gate to my grandfather's garden. My mother quickly switched off the only light that was on, and ran to open the back door.

"Thank God you're back!" said my mother as he came through the door. "I hope you're satisfied now!"

"Very." said my father closing the door behind him.

"Where did you go?" asked my mother. "Where…?"

"Switch on some light, give us a kiss and I'll tell you," he replied –obviously feeling very chuffed about having completed his night-time resistance effort.

"Did anyone see you?" asked my mother.

"No." answered my father shaking his head. "It's quiet and pretty dark out there – no sentries about either."

"Where did you go?" asked my mother.

"First I stuck one on Beauvoir's side door across the road – so the Jerries won't be able to miss it. Then I placed one with a stone on top of it in front of each of the houses up the hill behind us. And finally I put one inside the Jerry phone-box at the bottom of the drive across from Mourant's place – that'll give the guard something to read in the morning."

Coastal guns and bunkers

"Geoffrey," said my mother, turning to me, before I could ask any of my own questions, "It's late. Say good night and go back to bed."

My mother was not in any mood to hear my objections, so after saying good night I made my way back and crawled into bed wondering what Fritz would think should he be the one who found the British leaflet in the field phone-box.

In a defiant response to the Allied leafleted call for a German surrender, the Military High Command immediately hardened their stance by threatening to reduce the distribution of food to the civilian population, or force an evacuation. The Bailiff and the Superior Council, which included my grandfather, were shocked by the German threat and decided to send a letter of official protest via Baron von Aufsess' office to the German occupying forces, reminding them of their international obligation towards the civilian population.

~   ~   ~

Shortly after returning from my stay with Grumpa at Anneville Lodge, it became obviously apparent to those in charge that the Island was about to run out of gas supplies for both lighting and cooking. Those who were lucky enough to have them could return to the old Victorian wood- or seaweed-burning stoves. Provided, of course, they could find and gather the necessary fuel – cutting down or trimming branches off trees was strictly "verboten" by the military authorities, and those without such means, particularly those living in the town area, would have to find some other method by which to cook and provide themselves with a hot meal. There was great concern at the looming difficulties likely to arise for everyone, including the German garrison, should the coming winter be as cold as the previous one had been.

My father immediately decided that a partial solution to deal with the cooking problem would be to build three large communal brick ovens in the main warehouse at the factory. Ovens that would be large enough to accommodate the basic cooking needs of a number of local people within the surrounding neighbourhood. They could bring their pre-prepared evening dishes or whatever needed cooking into the factory in the morning and then pick it up in the late afternoon or after work and take it home, keeping everything warm, if not hot, in a simple hay-box that anyone with an inkling of skill could make for themselves. Hay- or straw-filled boxes were not new in Jersey. They were a very familiar item used for keeping freshly cooked meals warm, and for generations had been a part of most granite farmhouse and cottage kitchens.

While the whole idea was simple enough, it would, however, require a certain amount of effort in the way of organization and managing skills. The main problem for my father would be to persuade the German authorities to agree to the allocation and provision of enough bricks and mortar in order for him to build the ovens – not to mention the further difficulty in obtaining a special fuel permit in order to fire them. My father turned to Grumpa, who in turn, and on behalf of the Superior Council, spoke to Baron von Aufsess. Von Aufsess well understood the need for a balanced approach during a time of rapidly increasing shortages and uncertain difficulties on both sides, and dutifully granted a special permit.

Work on the ovens had hardly got under way when all gas supplies in Jersey were exhausted. Candles, firewood and what coal might still be found at the bottom of the fuel box hidden in the shed outside in one's backyard began to fetch a greedy premium on the black market.

By mid September we were back in class at school. Paper, pens, nibs, ink and pencils were also now in short supply and we had to learn to make use of every square inch of every sheet of paper we were given. None of us were allowed to sharpen our pencils on our own. When they became worn down, Miss Painter would carefully do the sharpening herself in order to avoid cutting away too much of the pencil during the process. The only thing that still remained in abundance was the sharp side use of her ruler cutting across our hands and fingers!

~   ~   ~

Despite all the difficulties and delays the ovens did finally get built. On the day when the ovens were opened up to the public, I hurried down to the factory after school with some of my mates so that we could see for ourselves how the whole operation was working. When we got there, some of the evening dishes had already been taken out of the ovens and were laid out ready for pick-up on a long, wide counter that had been set up behind a wire mesh barrier with three or four service windows. Each dish, saucepan or pot had a brass number tag on a wire attached to it, and people were already coming and going in a steady stream to claim and collect their evening meals.

Baron von Aufsess, accompanied by two of his aides, had also come to the factory to inspect the opening of the ovens. They were standing to one side and quietly observing while my father and Paul Boleat appeared to be explaining the details of the overall operation to them. Suddenly, the Baron looked up and, noticing me standing nearby with my friends, smiled and lightly tipped his cap as he had done when visiting Grumpa at Anneville Lodge. I returned his salute by politely tipping my school cap, as I would have for any other adult.

"You know him?" asked Drelaud.

"Yes." I replied. "I met him at my Grumpa's."

"What's his name?" asked Titch.

"Baron ... or Colonel something ..." I replied. "I can't remember, it's one of those long Jerry von 'Raus-Haus' names!"

"He's the one that rides the horse on the beach," remarked Drelaud.

"Yes! That's him!" said Titch excitedly in ready agreement. "I've seen him too."

I saw the same dark expression cloud my father's face as it had when I'd accepted the German officer's peppermint during the early part of the Occupation. Von Aufsess looked up again in my direction and said something to my father who responded with a slight nod before returning to the subject at hand.

"He must have said something about meeting me at Grumpa's house." I thought to myself, hoping nothing more would be said.

My father had built us two hay-boxes. One was made for general use in the kitchen, while the other one, slightly smaller, was fitted as a permanent fixture onto the front of his bicycle. At the end of the day at the office, my father would collect the cooked meal or whatever it was that my mother had pre-prepared for our supper, place it in the hay-box on the front of his bike and ride home as quickly as possible.

All in all, the whole arrangement did much to alleviate the sudden lack of cooking gas and the pressing needs being encountered by the civilian community. Still, my father was already having difficulties in acquiring enough coal to feed the factory's main boiler to provide steam for their other operations. Everyone knew that the greater test was yet to come when the cold weather of winter would arrive and fuel such as coal and wood for the public ovens would face further rationing in order to compete with the military needs of the Occupying forces.

~   ~   ~

20   Rationing and requisitions

Despite all our wartime troubles, September 1944 in Jersey continued to be sunny and warm, which helped retain some measure of cheerfulness and hope in the air. September also saw my eighth birthday come and go. My mother, like many others at the time, did her imaginative best with limited resources to throw a party for me. She organised a treasure hunt for us in the back garden. The treasure was a real George V silver shilling in a painted matchbox hidden in one of the rabbit hutches, a real prize that Nigel found before Elizabeth could get to it. Uncle Edward dropped in with a basket of ripe figs and gave me a British Royal Artillery cap badge to add to my collection.

Food was now in such chronic short supply, with open signs of growing malnutrition on both sides of the conflict, that whenever anyone was invited out to tea (brewed at best from bramble leaves) most people were expected to bring their own sandwiches to the event. However, on this birthday occasion, and much to our amazement, my mother and grandmother had got together to produce plenty of fruit jelly blancmange (made from carrageen seaweed) and a large, sugar-iced birthday cake made from carrots, coarse flour and home-dried raisins, with a cream centre and eight candles! The cake provided everyone with a taste to talk about at school for the rest of the month!

From my earliest recollections, September has always been a special time, for me, a season when I felt an unexplained sense of new beginning – not just for me or because my birthday happened that month, but for everybody. It's the time when the big high tides come, and that year I was hoping that the summer warmth in the seawater was going to reach over into early October, and with a bit of luck the Jerries would be hungry enough to allow everyone to go low tide fishing – I especially wanted to fish the gullies with Uncle Edward and Old Maurice, who knew all the special places – rocks and holes where a lobster or a good sized conger could be found.

~   ~   ~

Mrs Elliot arrived early each morning to help my mother look after the house, thereby affording my mother the extra time she needed in order to take care of Diana, my little sister. Mrs Elliot was a kindly soul. Her husband had left the Island to join the army just before the Germans arrived, and despite being left to face all the difficulties of the Occupation on her own, her cheerful countenance did much to brighten the darkest days for my mother.

Mrs Elliot, having worked a little longer than usual, was just about to leave for the day when my father arrived back from work with our evening meal. She immediately stepped in to help my father carry our supper from the hay-box on his bike where it had been kept snug and warm, to the hay-box in the kitchen. As it was getting late, my mother invited Mrs Elliot to stay and join us for supper.

We had barely sat down to eat our modest wartime meal when there came a knock on the back door.

"I'll go," said Mrs Elliot, moving to get up from her chair.

"No. Stay where you are," said my father, getting up from the table. "I'll see who it is."

But my mother was about to have none of it!

"I don't care who it is or how hungry they are," said my mother angrily. "You are not going back to the factory on any account – I've had enough of this!"

"All right, all right," said my father as he headed off and made his way through to the back door.

When my father opened the back door, he saw right away that it was the same man who had come on three prior occasions to ask him if he would go all the way back and open up the factory so that he could pick up his evening meal, and on three occasions my father had willingly abandoned his own supper to oblige the man for the sake of his family.

"I'm sorry," said my father. "I told you last time that it would be the last time – and so it was. In the future, you'll just have to be on time or have someone collect it for you. It's that or go without – I'm sorry!"

"But my kids haven't eaten all day." the man pleaded.

"That's your responsibility – not mine," said my father somewhat steadfastly. "Now, if you will excuse me, I have my own family to attend to."

"But, please!" cried the man desperately.

"I'm sorry," said my father beginning to close the door.

"You're a right bastard you!" yelled the man. "I'll get you for this you!"

After tolerating an additional burst of coarse verbal abuse, my father forcefully saw the man all the way to the garden gate before returning to the dining room. As he approached the table and was about to sit down, my mother looked at me…

"Stand up when your father comes to the table," she said forcefully. "Where are your manners?"

Realising that my mother was in no mood to be messed with, I began to get up.

"It's all right," said my father pulling his chair back. "Sit down."

I sat, and without any further word or comment from my parents, we continued with what was left of our evening meal in an uncomfortable silence.

~   ~   ~

Queuing for food rations in the Pollet, St Peter Port, Guernsey, 1944

Suddenly, without any warning, the German High Command ordered increased food requisitions for themselves and a maximum reduction in the distribution of food to the civilian population. The bread ration was cut in half, which came as a terrible shock to everyone. Signs of malnutrition had already begun to appear everywhere, to the point where a once-familiar face could be passed in the street without recognition. The elderly were especially affected; many simply fainted or died from a lack of nutrition. People who lived in town were especially hard-hit unless they had a friend in the farming community who might be willing to supply them with a few extra vegetables. Except for the odd rabbit, the meagre two-ounce weekly ration of meat simply disappeared and became totally unobtainable. Pet dogs and cats were snatched to fill Jerry stewpots. German soldiers were supplementing their main potato and cabbage diet with soup made from wild nettles and acorns. Fuel and food thefts of every kind on both sides of the Occupation fence were now increasing to the point where troops, having already been posted to guard fields both night and day, were now ordered to shoot to kill anyone pilfering, on sight and without warning!

It had finally come down to a case of either an impractical mass civilian evacuation of those not essentially engaged in the production of food, or severe food rationing. General von Schmettow, probably under orders from Berlin, had refused all approaches by Allied envoys to discuss any form of German surrender. Believing they could hold out until the May of 1945, mainly due to the good wheat harvest, the General refused to accept any further responsibility for the civilian population.

The Bailiff and the Superior Council immediately filed and delivered an indignant protest to General von Schmettow, citing the civilian food requisitions as a blatant violation of the Hague Convention. Von Schmettow immediately dismissed their objections, overriding the issue by justifying and citing the High Command's order as a "military necessity!" As a result the Germans launched a ruthless Island-wide search for food, confiscating any and all hoards of hidden supplies.

~   ~   ~

Elizabeth and I were playing up in the hayloft at Hamptonne when they came. At first I thought the sound of a large lorry rattling to a stop in the front yard might have been the milk lorry, come to pick up the cans, but Old Maurice and Charlie usually took care of that in the mornings. Scamp began to bark excitedly, loud enough to arouse the surrounding neighbourhood and even entice Old Pat into joining him.

Climbing down the ladder and running out into the yard, we found a group of Jerry soldiers piling out of a large, canvas-covered military lorry. Two of the soldiers were armed with casually slung rifles and stood back while the others set about unloading a number of empty boxes and barrels from the back of the lorry. A surly, stone-faced, junior-ranked officer carrying a clipboard stepped down from the cab of the lorry and looked about the yard.

Scamp continued to bark excitedly as he cautiously skirted around the intruders. Life for Scamp was very simple, if he couldn't eat it, chase it or play with it, then he peed on it! One of the unarmed soldiers made a vain attempt to befriend him, but the spritely terrier was having none of it. I managed to grab Scamp by the collar and pulled him to one side while Elizabeth ran to get his lead; neither of us wanted Scamp to end up in a Jerry stewpot.

Uncle Edward paused and took time to light his pipe before sauntering past the rose bushes in the front garden to where the Jerry officer was standing in the yard. After a few words, the officer followed Uncle Edward into the nearest storage barn where the seed potatoes were kept. There the officer began counting the stacked boxes of seed potatoes, carefully recording the total number down on his clipboard.

"What do they want?" I asked Uncle Edward.

"Their pound of flesh," answered Uncle Edward. "They're registering everything we have, and requisitioning whatever they want!"

"Requisition?" I asked. "What's that?"

"Taking half of everything we have," explained Uncle Edward. "In this case it means we'll have less to plant next season."

The officer ordered his troops to empty half the potatoes into their barrels and load them up onto the lorry and then, ignoring the five already registered milk-producing cows grazing down in the orchard, the stone-faced officer proceeded to search the entire property, noting down everything that could be eaten, stored or immediately requisitioned! It was very annoying to see the Jerries picking, and stuffing their tunic pockets with, apples and fruit right off the trees in the garden and the vines in the greenhouse.

When the Jerries had loaded up their lorry with whatever they were able to get their hands on, which also included a number of chickens, eggs, rabbits and even some of the swedes and mangels[23] that Elizabeth and I had helped Old Maurice to chop for the cows earlier that day before we went to play in the hayloft, the stone-faced officer signed and handed an itemised receipt to Uncle Edward.

"Take this into the depot in town," said the officer with a thick German accent, "and they will pay you, *ja*."

Uncle Edward glanced at the receipt, slowly turned it over in his hand, then very deliberately looked the officer up and down from cap to boots, before crumpling the receipt and dropping it like a piece of rubbish on the ground.

"Suit yourself," said the officer, turning to leave. "We have our orders. But …" he continued after pausing and turning back, "I would also remind you that you could still be shot for insulting the German Reich!"

"Perhaps so," said Uncle Edward, "but at my age I couldn't care less – in the end it will be our children who will see you and all your bloody commandants shot or swinging at the end of a rope!"

The stone-faced officer froze and turned white for a moment before wheeling on his heels without a word to board the lorry and drive off, throwing a very hostile look at Uncle Edward on the way.

"Do you think he will report you?" I asked.

"I doubt it," said Uncle Edward. "It may not be over for us yet, but the tide has changed for them – and they know it."

~   ~   ~

21 A Wölfle at the door

It was nearing the end of our summer holidays and my mother was busy altering some clothes so that I would have something to wear to school for the next term. The day started out for me as any other morning during the holidays. I got up, washed my face in cold water and tried using a pumice stone on my hands to do my part in saving what little soap was still available. I brushed my teeth with some new kind of wartime tooth powder that my mother had acquired, along with something else, in exchange for a small pair of fine lace curtains that could, she said, be turned into a couple of pairs of underwear. The tooth powder came in a little box divided into two sections. The left section contained a gritty white powder for cleaning that looked and tasted like a modern sink cleaner similar to Vim or Ajax, while the right section contained a finer, pink-coloured powder for polishing that tasted equally as bad, despite my mother sternly reminding me of how lucky we were to be able to acquire such an item.

By the time I arrived downstairs for breakfast with the gritty taste still in my mouth, my father had already left for the factory. For some reason that day, he had ridden off on his bike earlier than usual. In the meantime, I couldn't wait to get a sweeter taste in my mouth by putting a large dollop of sugar beet syrup on the coarse, husky porridge that Mrs Elliot always prepared when she arrived. I was expecting to meet Nigel and all our other friends at the rabbit patch in the front woods where we would decide how we were going to muck about for the rest of that day.

Frank Tanguy, our local milkman, arrived and poured two fresh pints of rationed milk from his traditional Jersey milk-can into a large pan, in which my mother or Mrs Elliott used to bring milk to a boil before leaving it to cool. This process allowed the rich Jersey cream to rise, settle and clot on the surface, to be used in place of butter, an item that had become barely available on the black market. My mother would always see to it that Frank, who worked very hard delivering milk, walking miles each day pushing a heavy milk cart, sat and had something to eat in the kitchen. She would ask Mrs Elliot to offer him a slice of coarse local bread, amply spread with clotted cream and, when available, a dollop of Uncle Edward's homemade jam on top – something Frank always seemed to look forward to on his rounds.

Before the war Frank, a simple, strong yet softly spoken man, had been a sailor in the Merchant Navy, and as he sat and rested that morning, he told me about all the different kinds of ships he'd served on, the foreign ports he had visited and all the raging storms that he had survived.

"Say thank you to your mum for me," said Frank as he gathered his cans and headed up the garden path. "Behave yourself *Mon Vier* – I'll see you Friday you ay."

I watched Frank walk up the garden path and waved to him as he closed the gate and headed off to make more deliveries before turning my thoughts again to playing with my friends in the front woods.

Hearing the front doorbell ring, followed by a loud knock, I turned and hurried back into the house making my way to the front hall, where my mother came to answer the door. When she did so, two plain clothed gentlemen and a Jerry soldier wearing a holstered sidearm confronted her.

"Mrs Norman?" asked one of the plain clothed visitors.

"Yes." answered my mother warily

"How do you do," he said cordially, "My name is Wölfle – we have come to search your house for a wireless set. It has been reported that you have one in your possession!"

With a sudden pounding in her heart, my mother quietly stepped back and allowed the men into the house.

Judging from the sound of his voice and the polite manner in which he spoke English, I immediately and naively took "Mr" Wölfle to be some kind of local official who was perhaps working for the States of Jersey. He was smartly dressed in a green Bavarian tweed jacket with a pair of matching baggy plus-four trousers. He spoke in proper, unaccented, cultured English and projected a casual air.

"And this," said Wölfle politely indicating the other man, "is *Abwehr* Officer Bohde."

Bohde, who wore a plain grey business suit, acknowledged my mother with a distant nod and nothing more. But for me, the sight of a Jerry soldier standing in our front hallway had totally absorbed my attention – so much so, that I hadn't grasped that "Mr" Wölfle and his friend were really Gestapo officers, or why they were here in the first place. After all, this was the first time a real live Jerry soldier had ever set foot in our house.

The soldier stood motionless, his eyes fixed in a glazed stare at the wall.

He looked like any other ordinary German conscript, with a standard issue bayonet slung from his belt; like all the others I'd ever seen, including the one hidden in the saddlebag on my bike, his had already flopped its way around to the middle of his back – where they were generally left to dangle and be forgotten. But for any small boy like myself at that time, the holstered sidearm on this soldier's belt made him much more interesting.

It was probably a larger type of Luger, I thought, loaded with real live oily brass ammo.

My mother called to me and suggested that I run along and play with my friends.

"No. No." said Wölfle, insisting politely. "I think it would be better if he stay – he can show us around."

Geheime Feldpolizei
The German Secret Field Police

Karl-Heinz Wölfle

Hauptmann (Captain) Bohde

So when the charming "Mr" Wölfle, in his fashionable tweed and baggy plus-fours softly suggested in his imperial English that I show him and his friend the way upstairs, I was more than happy to oblige!

Leaving the lone Jerry soldier, I led the two men upstairs, with my mother nervously following behind. As we neared the top of the stairs "Mr" Wölfle told me that he knew my father and that he had had the pleasure of officially meeting with my grandfather. Pausing to look about the upper hallway, the two men chose the first door on their left, which led into my parents' bedroom.

Excusing herself, my mother went into the playroom so that she could check on Mrs Elliot and Diana in her playpen. I followed the two men into the master bedroom and watched as they began to quietly search through all the cupboards and drawers, including my father's wardrobe.

After a moment or so, "Mr" Wölfle looked up from what he was doing and with a smile quietly asked me where I attended school.

"Victoria College Prep." I answered.

"Ah that is a good school," he said. "I believe Miss Cassimir is the head teacher up there – am I not right?"

"Yes," I said, "she teaches us French."

"And your favourite teacher?" he asked, while continuing to look through the various items he found in wardrobes and drawers.

"Miss Aubrey, I replied, "I like her the best – and Mr Nicolle!"

"Mr Nicolle?" he asked. "What subject does he teach?"

"Gym," I replied. "He teaches us gym and boxing."

"Boxing?" he repeated. "Really? Who else teaches you?"

"Miss Painter," I replied. "She teaches us most of the time."

"Do you like her?" he asked.

"Not as much as Miss Aubrey." I replied.

"Why is that?" he asked.

"Well, she's stricter than the others." I explained.

My mother appeared in the doorway and casually suggested that I might like to go back downstairs and talk to the soldier.

"You know how you like soldiers and that sort of thing," she said. "Perhaps he can speak English as well as these German gentlemen!"

Totally missing her point, I headed down to the front hallway and saw that the soldier had not moved from the place where he had first stood upon entering our home. Discovering that he couldn't speak a word of English, unlike Fritz or some others I had met, I gave up and went back upstairs.

When I got there, I saw that my mother had stepped across the hallway into the playroom to look in on Diana again. As I entered my parents' bedroom, "Mr" Wölfle and the other man were quietly exchanging some words with each other, but to my great surprise, they were both speaking in German!

"You're speaking German!" I exclaimed in astonishment.

"That's because we are German!" said "Herr" Wölfle, continuing what he was doing without looking at me.

Suddenly, a distant vibration of alarm began flooding through me. I thought of Miss Painter and what had happened to her father and brother

Peter – the deporting of father and eldest son to a concentration camp for violating German Occupational Law. I was an elder son!

"I thought you were…!" I began.

"Ah so," said Wölfle, with a faint smile. "You thought I was English – how interesting. No, I'm German!"

"But, you don't sound like one when you speak English!" I said.

"That's because I learnt my English in school when I was a little boy, just like you," he replied, while they both continued poking around in the wardrobe.

"Can you speak German?" Wölfle asked without looking up from what he was doing.

"No. But I know some German words." I replied.

"You do!" he said, pretending surprise with a slight smile and lifting his eyebrows, "Then tell me," he continued, "what words do you know?"

"*Scheisse* and *schweinhund!*" I said, knowing that I might well be courting an unpleasant response.

"Those are not nice words for little boys of your age to speak." He replied in a sudden un-rhythmic form of English.

"I know, but they are German words!" I declared, somewhat defiantly for having so stupidly taken him to be anything but a German.

"Where did you learn these words?" he asked, "Not from Miss Painter I hope?"

"No." I replied. "It's what we hear German soldiers saying all the time!"

Wölfle quietly continued with his search through the pockets of my father's suits until he came to a striped Harper Adams College blazer.

"Does your papa have a radio?" he asked, softly. "Does he keep a wireless set in the house?"

Suddenly realizing who they were and what they were looking for, my mouth felt uncomfortably dry.

"What if they find the bloody bayonet in my saddlebag?" I thought.

"No," I replied, somewhat nervously. "I don't know – what that is."

"Perhaps you could show me where he keeps it," he stealthily asked in a soft, cobra-like voice, without looking up.

"I don't know." I replied.

Fortunately, my mother returned to the bedroom and as she did, Wölfle suddenly came upon a single round of rifle ammunition in the pocket of my father's blazer! Wölfle held the round up to show Herr Bohde and after exchanging a few rapid words in German he turned to my mother.

"Where did your husband get this?" asked Wölfle, eyeing my mother suspiciously.

"Somewhere in the Far East – Malaysia I think. I don't know exactly," she replied feeling a little flustered. "He's had it for years – before we were married. It's nothing – it's just a pencil – it holds a pencil."

"A what?" questioned Wölfle, as he continued to examine the thing in his hand.

"It's a pencil," explained my mother with a nervous smile. "If you pull the pointed part off it you'll find a pencil inside."

Examining the round in his hand, Wölfle pulled the shell casing apart and unexpectedly saw that there was, in fact, nothing more than a small pencil inside. He looked at Bohde, and after exchanging a casual word or two in German, Wölfle, chuckling to himself, returned the bullet-encased pencil back into the pocket of the blazer and hung it back in the wardrobe.

Thoughts began to race through my mind. What if I hadn't taken my ammo collection to school to swap with Drelaud – what if they had found it in my satchel, and what if they found the bloody bayonet in my saddlebag?

Eventually, and after searching everywhere they could throughout the house without ripping the place apart, including my toy box in the playroom, they discovered nothing. For some reason they never bothered to search the loft, garage, potting shed or even the large walk-in henhouse, which I had briefly considered as a possible hiding place for my stuff.

Rejoining the Jerry guard at the foot of the stairs in the front hallway, Wölfle and Bohde exchanged a few words in German, appearing to be about to leave – as we were hoping they would.

"Are you sure, Mrs Norman?" asked Wölfle, closing in on my mother, studying her. "We know your husband kept two cars hidden at the canning factory. Fortunately, for him, the paperwork showed them as registered to the factory. Other than that, are you sure you haven't a wireless of any kind hidden in your house?"

"No!" said my mother. "I mean yes. I'm sure we have nothing like that here."

"You're sure?" questioned Wölfle.

"Yes, I assure you. Absolutely." answered my mother.

"It would not be good for your family if we came back and were to discover otherwise." he warned menacingly.

As young as I was, I could clearly read my mother's body language, and saw that she was growing extremely uncomfortable and anxious about something. Especially so when she turned to a bowl of fresh figs sitting on the hall table and, putting on a brave face, asked if they would like to try one.

"Thank you. No." said Wölfle, coldly eyeing my mother, waiting …

"If you go next door to Barry's house," I calmly suggested to Wölfle. "I know they have some cameras – in a box under Barry's bed!"

"Geoffrey!" exclaimed my mother.

"I wouldn't pay too much attention to that if I were you," said my mother with an apologetic smile, "he imagines more than he knows."

"No, not at all." said Wölfle. "Thank you, young man." He continued smiling down at me. "Thank you. You did the right thing."

Wölfle turned to Bohde, said a few words in German, and headed through the kitchen towards the back door, where he turned and paused after opening it.

"Thank you for your cooperation, Mrs Norman," he said. "We'll be on our way."

We watched in silent relief as Wölfle and Bohde hurried up the back garden path with the bored Jerry guard trailing along behind them.

As soon as Wölfle and his companions were out of sight and well away, my mother had a real go at me – up one side and down the other. She threatened to send me away to the boys' home at Gorey.

"Are you mad!" she yelled. "What's Madge going to say when she finds out that you turned them in like that? You know the Jerries always give out the initials of the informant! What in God's name were you thinking?"

She angrily went on to tell me that by having informed on a neighbour in such a way I had become a collaborator! And in doing so, I had let my family and the whole Island down!

I tried to explain to her that the cameras didn't work and were of no use and that I had just said what I had to in order to get them out of the house. But she was too upset, almost shaking with rage, to even remotely hear any kind of explanation upon my part, and despite the relief at seeing the back of the Gestapo, she obviously had other things on her mind.

"I need to talk to your father." she said, "Let's see if the phone is still working so I can get hold of him!"

Fortunately, the Jerries found nothing at Barry's house and were probably feeling a bit sick and tired of being led up the garden path by the many false, often spitefully incited leads that were being reported to them. Nevertheless, disturbing thoughts did linger and gnaw away at my gut for some time over the action I had taken, despite my well-meant intentions.

"What if my friends find out," I thought. There would be fist-fights, which

I was used to, but this time it would probably be more than one against me!

As soon as my father heard the news of the Gestapo's visit, he rushed home on his bicycle to console my mother. He assured me that I wasn't a collaborator and did his best to put my mind at rest by telling me that what I had done was well-intentioned, and not to worry about it.

But then came the bombshell of the day when he explained to my mother why he had left so early for the office that morning. Apparently, the crystal set that he had kept hidden in the cloakroom (something that I was not aware of) had not been working properly, and when he was unable to get the BBC News before breakfast that morning, my father had decided to take the set into the factory before anyone arrived and have Mr Mac repair it in the machine shop.

If there was ever a time in the life of our family that my mother could have strangled my dad and wiped the floor with him, well that was it. Boy-o-boy, did she explode!

At first I didn't know what to think. My mother's anger was quite justified under the circumstances, but there was something quite troubling about the whole affair. On one hand, I could admire my father's unrelenting defiance and resistance to anything German; I could even understanding him being mad at me for being friendly toward Fritz, but what if the crystal set had been in working condition and left in the cloakroom that morning. What if Wölfle, that Nazi swine, had found it. On top of which, there was the horrible question of who told the Gestapo that my father had a wireless. Why would anyone do that to us?

Shortly after the liberation in 1945, when Drelaud, Titch and I were idling about in the back garden, my father emerged from the house with a grey canvas bag – one I had never seen before.

My father put his hand into the bag, and to our astonishment, he withdrew several handguns, set them down on the back doorstep and invited us to hold and examine them.

Both my father and grandfather had willingly and defiantly held on to their firearms throughout the whole of the German Occupation, and both men were fully aware of the perilous risks involved. But when considering the fact that no one could imagine what actions one might have been "officially" called upon to carry out during the war, my grandfather had decided to keep two of his rifles wrapped in oilskin, and buried in a box under a pile of goat droppings in the goat shed up in the *côtil,* while my father had kept the forbidden handguns that were in his possession buried somewhere under the ground floor of our house, with access to them through a hidden trapdoor that he stealthily crafted under the lower end of the main stairwell.

"You mean you had them all the time!" I exclaimed to my father, "Even when the Gestapo were here!"

My father nodded slightly to the affirmative, but said nothing. Whether or not that was because he didn't want to say anything in front of my friends I can't say. But the awful thought that followed was what might have happened, had Wölfle and Bohde decided to rip up a few floorboards during their search, which quickly reminded me of Miss Painter and the terrible fate suffered by her father and brother.

I never ventured any further inquiry into whether or not my mother knew about any firearms being hidden under the house. Whatever might have been racing through her mind as Wölfle pressed her with those final questions before leaving, I simply did not want to know.

~ ~ ~

22 Baccie for souvenirs

The Etienne family lived next door to Nigel's house on the Inner Road, across from the manor's bull field. This large, mainly French-speaking family farmed the fields that ran behind both their house and Nigel's. Maurice Etienne, who attended another school, was the same age as Nigel and me, and we often played together in the front woods. One of the things I have always remembered about Maurice Etienne was how he had suffered more than anyone I knew during the previous winter with terrible chilblains on his hands and feet, and the fact that he hardly ever complained about it – he was a tough little blighter who grew up to spend much of his life serving the parish community.

We built a camp out of scraps of wood with a rusty corrugated iron roof behind the Etienne's front garage where we attempted to smoke our first cigarette. Maurice had pinched some of his grandma's substitute tobacco made out of dried rose petals that she smoked in a pipe, and using a piece of paper torn from the thin pages of a Bible, he twisted up our first smoke.

"No, you do it like this." explained Maurice exhaling some smoke through his nostrils. "It's easy."

So we tried and experimented in doing what we'd seen grown-ups doing until eventually all of us began to feel quite sick.

"My brother Denis says it's not the same with real tobacco," said Maurice, in an attempt to explain away the poor results.

One thing was for sure, I was not about to volunteer to tell anyone about the tobacco leaves that I was secretly drying on top of the wardrobe in my bedroom in order to find out.

Denis Etienne, Maurice's young teenage brother, was very good at experiments and making things. He built a bicycle for himself by taking the scrapped back end of an old discarded bicycle onto which he designed and attached a front axle with a set of homemade handlebars. The front wheel was much smaller than the rear, but it had a real pump-up tyre on it, which got him to school or into town and back. But the thing he was really good at was making miniature cannons out of empty rifle cartridge cases, and calcium

119

carbide bottle bombs. Denis would take some carbide, drop it in a small half-filled glass bottle of water, cork it, and then after counting to five would throw it as far as he could and wait for it to explode; all very fascinating for any seven- or eight-year-old to watch – and learn.

The best was when Denis taught us how to make a real miniature cannon that could be fired. Taking an empty cartridge case and boring a tiny primer-hole close to the base to create the cannon was the main part of the task. To this we added a variety of cannon mounts fashioned out of wood or wire, or simply gripped the cannon in a pipe wrench that we could stick into the ground.

Denis showed us how to use a thin bradawl to remove the bullet head and dig out the wads from a live round of Jerry ammunition. Then we emptied the gunpowder into a small pre-war tin tea box that we kept hidden up in the tree house. After pouring about an eighth of the original amount of powder into the cartridge cannon, wadding it down with a piece of paper or cotton wool, and loading a small ball bearing on top of it, we would head for the grassy rabbit patch in the front woods. We usually set the cannon up on or near the edge of the wall above the bull field and then, standing back, we would touch off the primer with a long taper for a mighty bang!

~   ~   ~

Disappointingly, I didn't get to go low tide fishing with Uncle Edward and Maurice. The lowest tides came during the midweek when we were at school, and there was no way my father would allow me to skip class after returning to school for the new term in order to go fishing. Nevertheless, Uncle Edward, Auntie Nan and Old Maurice managed to return with a healthy catch between them, including a variety of shrimp, lobster and spider crab, a couple of flat fish, some sand eels, and of course Old Maurice got a fair-sized conger. Despite having to give up a portion of the catch to the Jerry guards at the top of Le Hocq slipway, who also insisted on taking half of Old Maurice's conger, enough of the catch remained to share amongst family and friends. Of course Old Maurice wasn't too happy at losing half his conger, and according to Uncle Edward he swore like a trooper all the way up the lane until they arrived back at Hamptonne.

The Germans did allow some of the local fishermen to set low tide nets across the gullies, including the main gully down at Green Island, but unfortunately, as soon as the tide went out during the hours of curfew, the Jerries would always get there before the fishermen. Food and the shortage of such had become the main focus for the average Jerry soldier. One day, from Auntie Nan's garden above the beach, we watched as a couple of Jerries began shooting at seagulls with their rifles. They had climbed up on the wall surrounding the fortified four-barrelled 20mm Vierling anti-aircraft gun emplacement on Le Croc Point, and were taking pot shots at the gulls on the beach and nearby rocks until they managed to bag a couple.

"I don't think they taste too good," said Titch. "Not like pigeon or a blackbird or anything."

"Worse than eating an old crow," added Nigel.

"They're stringy and tough to eat," said Drelaud.

"How do you know?" I asked.

"My dad caught one out by our garage with a shrimpin' net," replied Drelaud. "My mum cooked it and it was bloody awful!"

Once the Jerries had collected their gulls and disappeared, we decided to go down and look around on the rocks below the barbed wire under the gun emplacement to see if we could collect any spent cartridges that they might have dropped from the wall above. Not only did we find a couple of empty cartridges, but we also discovered an absolute prize – a small open cardboard box with half a dozen live rounds left in it – needless to say, we certainly knew what to do with them!

~   ~   ~

October also saw an increase in German military activity. Jerry troops went on high alert, with a notable increase in their countryside manoeuvres. Troops were running around everywhere playing real soldiers in readiness for any sign of an airborne Allied invasion. The frightening thought of such an event ever happening did little to alleviate the growing anxiety of the civilian population. Everyone knew that an Allied invasion of the Islands would surely result in an awful bloodbath – on all *three* sides! Tensions continued to grow, and to make it worse we heard that the Germans had shot a young woman on the beach after curfew in what they said was an attempted escape.

Later that month it didn't get much better, when the Bailiff and the Superior Council were informed by the Germans that two French ladies[21] who lived in a house overlooking St Brelade's Bay had been arrested, tried by a military court and sentenced to death.

The women had circulated hand-made leaflets urging Jerry soldiers to shoot their officers. Naturally, this disturbing news spread through the civilian

---

21 Artists Lucy Schwob (aka Claude Cahun) and her stepsister Suzanne Malherbe (aka Marcel Moore), who were both Jewish, who had come from France to live in Jersey in 1937.

community like a plague, causing much distress. I particularly remember my mother being quite upset after hearing about the harsh sentence pronounced upon them.

Worried that the Jerries would actually carry out the sentence and shoot these two ladies, I got out of bed and crept to the top of the stairwell so that I could overhear my parents discussing the matter while they sat below in the dining room.

"Surely," argued my mother, "they can't allow such a thing to happen."

"They certainly can," replied my father. "The blighters hold all the guns and can still do whatever they want."

"What does your father have to say about it?" asked my mother.

"Well, he told me the Bailiff was attempting to formally intervene with the High Command on behalf of the two sisters," answered my father. "Warning the Jerries that if they start executing women in Jersey, they run the risk of causing civil unrest – something they don't really need right now."

"But, what if…?" began my mother, thinking aloud.

"Look," said my father. "One thing's for sure, had they been caught before we got cut off from France, they would have been shipped out and put up against a wall and shot as soon as they landed there – it's hard to say what they'll do now."

"Is that all your father had to say?" asked my mother.

"He said he's spoken to the *Kommandant*, von Aufsess … the Baron," began my father,

"And …?" asked my mother.

"Well, he told me that the Baron, as a German officer, had little sympathy for the women."

"Why?" asked my mother. "Because they're French?"

"No. Not that." said my father. "He was speaking as a soldier concerning what they had done – they were inciting mutiny. But …" continued my father, "Grandpa said that the Baron was also in agreement that they shouldn't start executing women in Jersey, so the council is hoping that between him and the Bailiff they can persuade those at the top not to do anything rash."

Fortunately, the Germans did listen to the Bailiff and commuted the sentence on the women to life imprisonment, perhaps doing so more in the light of their strategically impotent military situation rather than as an act of compassion, or to save face.

While all this had been going on, the Jerries, including Fritz's unit (who were all billeted up in the two houses above Callec's field to the rear of ours)

had also been busy setting up three huge roll-bombs to guard the approach to the large-calibre gun hidden inside the octagonal hut up on Mount Ube overlooking the quarry. One Saturday morning, natural born curiosity saw Nigel, Drelaud, Titch and I venturing up the steep pathway running along the edge of the quarry face that led toward the ancient dolmen just above the big gun emplacement. On our way up the pathway, I picked up a long stick and began to whack aimlessly at some of the overhanging bushes bordering the top of the quarry until we unexpectedly stumbled upon a newly-dug wickerwork-lined slit-trench – complete with a Jerry guard sitting in it! My stick had accidently landed on the back of the Jerry guard's helmet with an awful clang! The guard, who at the time had been looking up through a pair of binoculars, was as much surprised and embarrassed as we were with our sudden and unexpected encounter. Under a barrage of angry German profanity that could be heard for miles around, we turned and ran back down the pathway as fast as we could, hoping that we wouldn't get shot!

~   ~   ~

One morning while I was sitting alone up in the tree house, half expecting Nigel to turn up so we might go and mess about together, I noticed an older, grizzle-haired off-duty Jerry soldier strolling down the lane in my direction. Although I had never spoken with him, I had often seen him in the neighborhood and knew that he, like Fritz, lived in one of the houses above Callec's field. He stopped almost directly below, on the other side of the lane from where I was, and began rummaging through the undergrowth of the hedge that ran along the top of the wall bordering the lane. After selecting some bits of dried fibrous mulch, he turned, and leaning back against the wall, took a pipe out of his tunic pocket and began to fill it. After lighting his pipe and taking several obviously unsatisfactory puffs, he tapped and emptied the pipe out against the wall. Looking about for another solution he found a piece of twig and began to shave it into the bowl of his pipe with a penknife – but this too was to prove as chokingly unpalatable for him as his prior experiment.

Giving up any further attempt to fill his pipe, the grizzle-haired Jerry continued on his way down the lane. I hurriedly climbed down from the tree house and headed for the top of the wardrobe in my bedroom where I had stashed the trove of honest-to-God real tobacco leaves.

"Where are you going?" asked my mother as I ran up the stairs.

"To get something to play with from my room," I yelled back.

"Well, wipe your feet in the future before you come in," she cried. "I've got enough dust in the house without you trampling in any more! Do you hear me?"

"All right," I yelled back.

"Besides I don't want you running in and out of the house all day – do you hear me?"

I turned to make sure that she wasn't following me upstairs "Yes," I replied. "Yes, I heard you."

The tobacco leaves had dried quite well into a varying array of light brownish shades and even, to both my surprise and delight, smelt like tobacco. I climbed down from the chest of drawers and carefully placed the leaves inside my shirt under my sweater and smoothed everything down. I grabbed a round pre-war lozenge tin in which I kept some duplicate cigarette cards for swaps at school, my sheath knife that Uncle Edward had given me for Christmas, and headed back downstairs on my way to the tree house where I could sort things out without being disturbed.

Passing my mother on my way out of the house, she looked up from filling a bowl with some fresh apples that Uncle Edward had sent over, and seeing the sheath knife stuck in my belt and the round lozenge tin in my hand, asked me what I was up to.

"Nothing much," I replied. "I just want to sort out some of my swapping cards."

"Mind what you get up to with that knife," she said. "And stay out of trouble!"

"Can I have an apple?" I asked.

"Here," she replied, handing me one. "Chew it properly or you'll get a stomachache."

Returning to the seclusion of the tree house, I removed the tobacco leaves from inside my shirt and, setting a leaf off to one side, I rolled up the remaining eleven as tightly as I could into a sausage-like roll. I then began slicing and chopping up the roll on the wooden floor of the tree house with my sheath knife. Soon I had what must have been a crude pile of coarse pipe tobacco, but real tobacco nonetheless. Dumping my duplicate cigarette cards out of the lozenge tin, I filled it with the chopped tobacco. Before closing the tin, I cut a slice out of my apple and placed it in the tin together with the chopped tobacco – a trick I knew Uncle Edward employed in order to keep the tobacco in his pouch moist and thereby prevent it from drying out too much.

After lunch, Nigel turned up at the tree house and I showed him my tin of rough-cut baccie.

"Are you going to smoke it," asked Nigel.

"No," I replied. "I'm going to show it to Fritz and see if he will swap me for a Jerry forage cap – or something."

"What if he doesn't smoke?" asked Nigel.

"They all smoke," I replied. "If he doesn't, then I'm sure he'll know another Jerry who does."

"See if you can get an officer's cap from him or one of those Jerry rucksacks with a fur hide cover," he suggested.

"Well, that might be a bit difficult," I said. "But if you come with me, we might be able to get him to add an officer's silver breast eagle for you." I offered.

"As well as the forage cap for you?" he asked.

"Yes," I replied, "you never know …"

We ran up the lane only to find another guard, one I had not seen before, on duty at the bottom of the long driveway.

"*Wo ist Fritz?*" I asked.

"*Fritz?*" he questioned. "*Wissen Sie Fritz?*"

"*Ja, Fritz,*" I replied. "*Wo ist?*"

"*Fritz beim hier um sechzehn uhr,*" he replied, holding up four fingers and pointing to his watch. "*Heute nachmittag* – afternoon ja?"

"*Vier,* four – this afternoon *ja?*" I asked in an attempt to confirm what I thought he was saying.

"*Ja vier* – four," he said after pausing for a moment to look us up and down. "*Wo sprechen Sie mit Fritz* – why you want Fritz?"

"*Nichts als, nur,*" I said beginning to feel a little ill at ease with his piercing gaze. "Nothing – *nichts. Danke* – thank you," I said to the guard.

I turned and began heading back down the lane towards the tree house.

"Why don't we show him the baccie?" asked Nigel as he ran to catch up with me.

"No," I replied. "It's safer to wait for Fritz."

"Safer! Why?" asked Nigel.

"Because," I began slowly, in an uncertain attempt to explain. "I don't know … I don't like this Jerry. He's not like Fritz – if we showed the baccie to this bugger he could just take it and then we'd be … what could we do …?"

We returned to the tree house and decided to sit and wait until Fritz came on duty. Having referred to the Jerry guard the way I did as being a "bugger" gave Nigel pause.

"Do you think it's a sin to swear?" he asked.

"I don't know," I answered. "Maybe it is or my dad wouldn't clout me so hard every time he or my mum caught me doing it."

"But, do you think God gets angry at us when we swear?" asked Nigel earnestly emphasizing the word God.

"Yes, well I've wondered about that too," I said.

"But, do you think when He hears us He counts all of them up?" asked Nigel intently. "Do you think He counts them up against us?"

"I imagine He does," I said. "Reverend Labey says God even knows what we think! Even before we say anything!"

"Even if we just think of a swear word – He knows?" questioned Nigel.

We were quiet for a moment. It just seemed a whole lot more than I was able to fathom at the time.

"How many bad words, including the one you just called that Jerry, have you ever said?"

"I don't know," I answered. "I don't think I've said that many ... Not like Drelaud and some of the other kids. I mean, Drelaud says 'bugger this' and 'bugger that' and 'bloody hell' all the time, and even some other words."

Certainly, words I was not about to repeat given the context of our discussion. This was, after all, quite a question for us and it was hard for anyone to know what God might really be thinking, but one thing we both knew: Michael Drelaud was definitely on his way to hell.

~ ~ ~

Fritz was sitting on the granite steps below the closed gateway leading into the back woods when we arrived later in the afternoon. He was looking through his little red dictionary and, having removed his heavy helmet, I noticed the top of his tunic was casually unbuttoned. Something about the worn out way in which he was sitting there seemed to say that he just didn't care anymore if he got caught by an officer or some grumpy sergeant. By then it did appear as though many of the regular Jerry conscripts were tired and totally fed up with the war, and wanted nothing more than simply to go home to their families.

"Ah! Jeffie, Nigel," said Fritz looking up from his dictionary to greet us with a tired, but cheerful smile. "You *gut* today *ja*?"

"*Ja*," I replied with a nod. "*We gut und Sie*?"

"*Ja* – me *gut*," he replied.

I pulled out the round lozenge tin from under my sweater and began to pry open the lid.

"Ah … *vas gebs hier*?" asked Fritz as he stood up, put away his dictionary, slung his rifle and generally straightened himself out. "What you have here?"

"Tobacco. *Rauchen*," I said, lifting the piece of apple off the cut tobacco and holding it up for him to see.

"*Ah so!*" said Fritz, lifting his eyebrows then looking up the driveway to make sure no one else was looking at us. "Tobacco, *ja*?"

I handed the leaf to Fritz, which he then held up to his nose and took a good sniff.

"*Ja. Das ist gut rauchen!*" he said taking another good sniff. "We make … we do *Geschäft* … business *ja*?"

The sound of an approaching staff car immediately caught Fritz's attention.

"*Schnell*! Quick!" said Fritz urgently handing the leaf back to me, before putting his helmet on, straightening his tunic and running over to his post near the field telephone box. "You go now … *ja … und morgen …* tomorrow *ja …* we make *gut* business!"

The next morning I got up, and after a quick breakfast with my dad, I immediately ran upstairs and began to get ready for school. Knowing that Fritz would be on duty by eight o'clock, and not wanting to be late for class, I waited until I heard my father tap the hallway barometer – something he did every day before leaving for his office. Then, with the coast clear, I grabbed the tobacco-filled lozenge tin from the top of my wardrobe, put it in my satchel with my schoolbooks, yelled goodbye to my mother on the way out of the house and headed for my bike.

Fritz reached into the hedgerow behind the field phone-box and pulled out a small knapsack that he had obviously hidden there. After a quick glance to see that no one was about, he produced the forage cap I had so longed for, a belt complete with buckle, an ammunition pouch and a lovely pair of silver *Oberstleutnant*'s shoulder boards which I would give to Nigel in lieu of a silver breast eagle. That, Fritz explained, would take a little more time to get. Happily, I handed him the lozenge tin, stuffed the souvenirs into my satchel, said goodbye to a broadly smiling Fritz, and took off for school like a rocket – the slickest swapper and the richest eight-year-old on the Island!

~   ~   ~

By the end of October the food shortages throughout the Islands were moving towards an even more alarming level. And although my parents, just like those of my friends, generally avoided mentioning too much of anything in front of us, we children were all well aware of their growing concerns.

While on his way into town to attend to States business, my grandfather stopped at the house on one of his early morning visits. My father had already left for his office, and although I was about to head off for school, I wanted to hang about and spend a few minutes or so with Grumpa so that I could hear some of his latest news.

On this occasion he mentioned to my mother that the Superior Council had drafted and submitted a communication to the German High Command via Baron von Aufsess, requesting permission to seek Red Cross relief for the civilian population via international diplomatic channels.

"Will they allow that?" asked my mother hopefully.

"We don't know for sure," said my grandfather cautiously. "Von Aufsess says they can do nothing without Berlin's approval – we'll just have to wait and see."

"God, something has to be done," said my mother. "Especially now, without any supplies coming in from France. We can't go on like this much longer."

"I know," agreed my grandfather. "But we are hopeful, because under international treaty the Germans have a responsibility to provide for the civilian population."

"What! By running around requisitioning everything?" said my mother with an air of frustration creeping into her voice. "Just ask your brother Edward about it!"

"I know," said Grumpa softly. "But allowing Red Cross aid into the Island will mean just as much to the Jerries as it does to us – even the Nazi hardliners like Admiral Hüffmeier know this."

"God – I hope you're right!" said my mother. "But, how long will it take?"

"Well, it will depend on what Berlin has to say," explained Grumpa, "and London will also have to agree ..."

"London?" asked my mother. "To agree?"

"Yes. Both sides must agree not to blockade the relief and allow it to get through to us," he explained.

"But, surely they ..." my mother began.

I wanted to stay and hear more of what Grumpa had to say, but my mother insisted I get going on my bike or be late for school.

The road along the back of the golf course had become an obstacle course of large potholes, with little hope of ever being repaired until after the war – I dreamed of a day when we'd be able to ride on a smooth roadway with real pump-up tyres; my hosepipe substitutes had started to thump at the joint again – irritating me no end. Nevertheless, as I rode and thumped my way to school that morning, I tried to sort out in my mind what Grumpa had been explaining to my mother concerning the Red Cross thing.

~   ~   ~

Much to everyone's relief, Berlin agreed to permit negotiations for civilian food assistance to proceed through international channels – a renewed breath of hope.

It wasn't until some time after the war that we were able to fully learn the details of how the request for relief was received and dealt with by the British Cabinet. Apparently, when the British Government was informed, via the Red Cross, of the chronic food shortages in the Channel Islands, Churchill stubbornly dismissed all thoughts of allowing a civilian evacuation, or permitting any Red Cross relief to get through to the Islands. Instead, Churchill was of a mind to use our condition to pressure the Germans into either keeping their international obligations to the Islanders, or accepting an outright surrender. This was, with hindsight, an unfortunate decision that did no more than prolong the suffering for everyone.

~   ~   ~

23   A goat in the garage

November saw the weather turn colder, with shorter hours of daylight heralding the approach of winter. Beside increases in rationing, the population also had to put up with massive German requisitions of Island food supplies. Without any news of relief in sight, the day-to-day struggle to survive was becoming critical. Medical supplies and hospital services were almost at a distressing standstill. Insulin had all but run out, and many patients died. Fuels were at an all-time low and my parents, like everyone else, were now looking at an end to our supply of electricity. The desperate plight of the civilian population had long turned to prayer for our survival or for some half-hearted miracle that our situation might somehow be relayed to the British Government via the few Islanders who were willing to risk their lives in an escape to France.

Although hardliner Nazis like Admiral Hüffmeier, who was headquartered in Guernsey, showed no signs of ever capitulating or surrendering, the Islands had for all intents and purposes become no more than a giant prisoner of war camp. Except for limited flights between the Islands and Berlin, and despite holding some very big coastal guns against invasion, the German forces, though well armed and stocked with munitions, were basically going nowhere.

Some of the other senior German staff officers like General von Schmettow, Colonel Heine, von Helldorf and von Aufsess were well aware and civilised enough to recognise this fact. They had all studied the military theory of Carl von Clausewitz, the German-Prussian soldier who had stressed in his most notable work, *Vom Kriege: The Moral and Political Aspects of War*, "A war once lost should not be further protracted." If only they and Churchill could have conferred, but that wasn't to be.

~   ~   ~

Unlike most houses along the Inner Road, Nigel's still had a small piece of lawn in the front garden that had somehow avoided being used to grow vegetables. We both liked to play field hockey, and the little piece of lawn in their front garden was an ideal place for us to practice on. Nigel had a good pre-war cricket ball without too many scratches on it, which he kept, together with a couple of hockey sticks, in their garage. One day, leaving the others to continue playing in the front woods, Nigel and I decided to head back to his place and play hockey on their lawn. When we got there, Nigel swung the folding garage door back, and to our surprise we found ourselves looking into the eyes of a white goat that was calmly resting on a pile of loose straw in the middle of the garage floor.

"Close the bloody door!" cried Nigel's father running out of the front door of their house followed by another man whom neither of us knew. "Close the door before anyone sees!"

After closing the garage door, we petted the friendly goat and asked where it had come from and what it was doing there.

"Never you mind," said Mr Meeks. "We're going to slaughter it for meat! You can both go and play elsewhere or you can stay here and watch – so make up your mind!"

We elected to stay and watch. After all, Uncle Edward had allowed me to watch a calf being born in the stables, so why not this? I thought.

The two men set about clearing the top of a large wooden chest before lifting the goat onto it and placing the animal on its side and binding its hooves together with a piece of light rope. Surprisingly, apart from the odd bleat, the goat offered very little in the way of resistance.

Mr Meeks took hold of the goat and held it down in place. After a quick exchange of gleeful glances with each other over the fact that they were on to something illicitly tasty during a time of such chronic shortages, the other man took what looked to be no more than a six-inch kitchen knife and slowly stuck it into the side of the animal's neck. Nigel and I watched uncomfortably as the goat began to bleat in pain as the man wielding the knife crudely probed the side of the animal's neck, searching for whatever it was that he had in mind. As young as Nigel and I were, it was obviously clear to both of us that neither of these two men knew what the hell they were doing.

"Stop!" cried Nigel "You're hurting it!"

"It will be over soon," said the man as he wiggled and twisted the knife about in the goat's neck. "I'm just trying to find its spinal cord so I can cut it!"

Eventually after much bleating on the part of the poor goat, the man finally succeeded in getting his blade between the vertebrae in the neck and snapping its spinal cord. By then, Nigel and I had had enough. Old Maurice was disgusted when I told him how Nigel's dad and his friend had butchered the goat.

"Silly sods them ay," said Maurice casually. "Them kind knows nothing about them things ay. Lucky the Jerries didn't catch them with it. When you slaughter an animal ay *mon vier*, you must bless it first and do it quick."

"What do you mean ... bless it?" I asked.

"Ah, *mon vier*," explained Maurice, "you must give thanks to God first you, and then ... one quick sharp slice right through and you let 'em bleed ay. That way they feels nothing them – Me and Charlie, we done it many times us."

~   ~   ~

One morning we woke up to find that two of our chickens and three of our rabbits were missing. Someone had stolen them during the night! My mother was more than just furious; she was raving mad! We were now virtually out of food and supplies.

"For God's sake!" she cried, "I hardly know where our next meal is going to come from – and now this."

Left with one old rabbit and three chickens that weren't laying due to a lack of proper feed, my father decided it would be better to eat the rabbit while we still had one and take the remaining chickens over to Hamptonne where Uncle Edward was better equipped to look after them until such time as they started laying again.

My father drove two nails into the upper doorframe of the potting shed to which he then strung the old rabbit up by its hind legs. Before I could say anything, he stepped back and hit the rabbit in the back of its head with his fist! The rabbit died instantly. Blood ran from its nose and we quietly waited until the last drop drained out.

The hardest part of the entire task came when skinning the animal. To do this, my father had to hold onto a corner of the pelt and pull with all of his weight drawing the fur back and down towards the head.

He had certainly done a better job of painlessly dispatching the rabbit than Nigel's father had done with the goat in their garage.

At the same time I thought it rather a shame that we hadn't taken a moment to bless the old rabbit in the way I'm sure Old Maurice would have done – unless it was only goats, sheep and cows that were supposed to be blessed before being slaughtered. Nevertheless, when we sat down at the dining room table and said grace, I did remember to thank God for the old rabbit.

24   Oranges and roll-bombs

As we moved into December, I had taken to wearing my rubber wellingtons to school with two pairs of socks on the inside. Grandma had knitted me a pair of gloves without fingertips to keep my hands warm in class. I also wore these underneath another pair of gloves when I rode my bike to school – still my hands and feet were always half-frozen, and wearing short trousers in those days also meant that we all arrived with red-raw knees to boot. Even Fritz took to stamping his feet and wearing a grey scarf under his cold steel helmet, knotted under his chin and with the ends tucked into the top of his greatcoat.

At the beginning of the term we had moved from our old classroom, located at the top of the building, down to a ground floor room situated directly across from Miss Cassimir's study – making it harder for us to muck about between classes. The room was bigger, and despite the iron-grated fireplace, it was much colder! My desk was towards the back of the room, right next to a window that was exposed to the cold east winds.

Every so often during classes, Miss Painter would allow three or four of us in turn to huddle around the fire for a few minutes to warm ourselves up. Fuel was almost non-existent, and whatever was available remained strictly rationed. So some of us, that is to say anyone who could find, obtain or spare such, would bring a small piece of coal or anthracite wrapped in old newspaper to school, and any other form of fuel, including twigs or peat moss, that could be used to keep the classroom a little warmer. A small piece of coal would go a long way towards keeping one well in with Miss Painter.

> *Christmas was coming and the goose was getting fat,*
> *Please put a penny in the old man's hat.*

Unfortunately, we all knew that unless you could find one on the black market, there would be no goose for anyone that year. Instead, everyone would have to make do and be thankful for whatever morsel or blessing, if any, might happen to come his or her way. Nevertheless, as we approached the end of the term, like most kids we still looked forward to the coming Christmas holidays.

Much to our delight, Miss Painter issued us with an extra clean sheet of fresh paper, out of which she instructed us to make a special Christmas card. Enthusiastically, we all took up the task as a welcome relief from the normal academic grind of the school week.

"Now," she said sternly, "I want you to draw and colour a Christmas card for someone who is not as fortunate as you are. Someone," she continued, "who doesn't have a family, relative or friend to remember him or her during the holiday."

After a moment of thoughtful enquiry about the idea, a number of interesting choices began to emerge. Everyone from one end of the class to the other seemed to know of some old lady, man or couple that lived alone in a nearby cottage or home that they passed on their way to school each day.

"What about some of the orphaned boys at the boys' home?" suggested Bob Sowden raising his hand. "I bet they would like to get a Christmas card – from someone."

"That's a good suggestion, Robert," agreed Miss Painter as she placed the one communal box of colouring crayons that we all shared on the front of her desk. "Choose any person you like. Now get on with it. Use one crayon at a time and don't argue over them."

Drelaud announced that he was going to draw and colour a Christmas card for Old Barney Quinn – a choice that seemed quite funny at first. After all, everybody knew Old Barney Quinn. He was a veteran of the First World War, a soldier who had been badly shell-shocked and was often seen wandering around town on his own wearing a pair of hobnailed boots and a navy-blue roll-neck sweater. To all intents and purposes he seemed like any other normal elderly person until suddenly, and without any warning, he would start gesturing and dancing in the most extraordinary manner right in the middle of King Street. For a moment and without any doubt, Barney Quinn would cut an extremely ridiculous, yet comic picture of himself. But everyone knew how badly Old Barney had been injured during the war, and didn't give it much thought, leaving the passing Jerry soldiers in the street hard-pressed to make any sense of the strange and unexpected spectacle.

I had often stopped and spoken with Old Barney on my way through town, and he always seemed a very polite and considerate person – until he started dancing. So perhaps Drelaud did have a noble thought or two in choosing Barney for his Christmas card effort.

It was cold outside, so the first person I thought of sending a Christmas card to was the poor Czechoslovakian man, the forced labourer that I had seen so badly beaten up by the OT supervisor, and his fellow prisoner, the one with the tarred feet. Surely, no one could have been any worse off than those poor fellows. Then Fritz the guard came to mind. I thought perhaps that I could draw a picture of a cottage somewhere in a forest under a deep blanket of snow with smoke rising from its chimney and put "Happy Christmas" in red across the sky above and make believe that the Christmas card came from his wife and baby son. Had my father ever found out that I had had so much as a thought of doing such a thing, he would have knocked my head off. In the end, I simply settled for drawing the cottage snow scene and would decide to whom I would send it later.

I thought it would be nice to see a yellow lantern or a warm candle glow in one of my cottage windows. All the yellow crayons were being used by others, so I tried looking for an orange one instead, but found none.

"You can have this one," offered Titch. "I'm almost finished with my orange bits."

Titch was good at drawing stuff. He had drawn a picture of a decorated Christmas tree by a window looking out onto a frosty snow scene. The tree had yellow candles on the end of its branches and an angel with wings on top. Underneath his tree, he had drawn a number of brightly-coloured wrapped presents.

"What are those?" I asked, pointing to some ball-like things hanging on the end of a couple of branches.

"They're oranges," he said, handing me the orange crayon

"But oranges don't grow on Christmas trees," I said.

"Well I know that silly," he said. "They're just there for decoration until after you've opened all your presents, then you can eat them."

"Have you ever tasted one?" I asked.

"No," he said somewhat distantly, "but I will after the war."

"Oranges?" I questioned. "On a Christmas tree?"

"Yes," he said somewhat more affirmatively. "That's how my mum said it was – before the war."

Miss Painter got up from her desk and began to make her way through the classroom, checking as she passed on the various artistic Christmas card efforts that were in full progress. When she got to Titch's desk, she told us to stop talking and for me to get back to my desk and work on my own card or she'd give me some arithmetic to do instead!

The distracting thought of hanging oranges on a Christmas tree was new to me, and for a moment I had all but forgotten about why I had wanted to get hold of a yellow or orange crayon in the first place. Returning to my desk I sat down and was about to get back to the business of creating a glow in one of my Christmas card cottage windows when …

"What in God's name do you call that?" Miss Painter angrily demanded, standing at Drelaud's desk.

Everybody stopped what they were doing and looked up to see what was going on. I saw Miss Painter's lips react and tighten into her standard "mean and serious look" that she took on when her patience wore thin.

"What?" asked Drelaud, looking up at Miss Painter as though butter wouldn't melt in his mouth.

"That there?" she asked demandingly. "What's that?"

"A roll-bomb!" answered Drelaud.

"A roll … And what are those things?" she demanded.

"Jerry hand grenades!" said Drelaud.

"Really!" she said. "And you think that's funny, do you?"

Before Drelaud could answer, Miss Painter hauled off and gave him such a clout across his right ear that he almost ended up on the floor beside his desk.

For a moment it looked as though Drelaud was about to pay a visit to the back room and bend over for six, instead, Miss Painter ordered him to stand in the corner until it was time to go home!

"This is not funny," said Miss Painter, holding up Drelaud's paper card and artwork for all to see – before angrily tearing it up.

Drelaud had drawn and coloured a Christmas tree, but instead of having a star or angel on top, it had a Jerry helmet, with several hand grenades dangling from its branches and a large roll-bomb sitting under the tree with a red ribbon tied around it!

~   ~   ~

I was glad when we finally broke up from school for the Christmas holidays. My report card was not the best on record, but it was good enough to avoid any threats of a "no Father Christmas this year" or being packed off to the boys' home where I might have become a co-recipient of Bob Sowden's charitable Christmas card.

As the December weather continued to get stormier and much colder, Mrs Elliot would clean the grate and light the fire in the dining room as soon as she arrived in the morning. With no gas for the main stove and the supply of electricity cut to a couple of hours during the day, the dining room fireplace became our main, if not our only source of heat within the house. It had been designed with water pipes running behind the firewall so that as long as we were able to find enough fuel to burn, it would provide us with a modest amount of hot water beside being able to keep at least one room in the house warm.

On cold nights, I would take my clothes off and carry them into bed with me, where I could keep them warm under the eiderdown. In the morning when I got up, my shirt, sweater, pants, and socks would be nice and warm when I put them on again. They may well have been wrinkled, but they certainly made do for mucking about during the holidays, not to mention a more comfortable start to the day.

Shortly before we had broken up for the school holidays, rumours of Red Cross relief had begun to spread through the community. Finally, on 13 December, the Bailiff published an official announcement stating that the British Government had agreed to allow a Swedish Red Cross relief ship to leave Lisbon, Portugal in about a week and head for the Channel Islands, and that it would be carrying a shipment of food and essential relief supplies – but was it really true! How long would it take to arrive? If only it could arrive before Christmas! These were the thoughts and questions on everyone's lips. Moreover, even though Grumpa had assured my parents and others that all the diplomatic arrangements for the relief were in place and truly underway they, like everyone else, would continue to hold their breath until it appeared on our desperately hungry horizon.

In the meantime, rations and food supplies were down to a bare minimum, and without the provision of our school lunches during the holidays, my mother decided to feed me my main meal of the day at lunchtime, along with my little sister, rather than have us wait until suppertime when my father came home in the evening.

"I have absolutely nothing left to offer your father for supper when he gets home from work this evening!" cried my mother in despair before running out of the room and taking Diana with her.

For a brief moment while I sat there alone with my half-eaten meal, I frighteningly thought for a moment that she was blaming me for the situation, but of course, that was not the case. I knew she had run out of ration coupons and was upset because she would be unable to acquire any further food rations for either love or money until the beginning of the following week!

Later that evening I sat at the dining room table and watched as my father spread some clotted cream onto one of two thin slices of coarse bread, which he then topped off with a little sugar beet syrup. It was all he was going to get to eat that evening and I knew it was not the first time that my parents had had to hold back on feeding themselves for the sake of Diana and I. I tried as we sat there together to think of something cheerful to say to my father, but I just couldn't come up with anything.

25 Christmas 1944

On Thursday, 21 December, my grandfather called in at the house on his way home from town to let my mother know that the Germans had informed the Superior Council that the Swedish Red Cross relief ship had left Lisbon and was on its way, heading for the Channel Islands.

"I'd say it should be here by the end of the month," said Grumpa.

"The end of the month?" questioned mother.

"Yes," answered my grandfather assuredly. "It should be here by then. In fact, now that we know it is on the way I've decided that we will have one of the goats for Christmas this year – time we all had a proper meal."

It had indeed been a long time since anyone had been lucky enough to have eaten fresh meat, and the very thought of it, combined with the news of a Red Cross ship heading our way, did much to spread some eager anticipation for a festive celebration through the entire family. It was particularly good news for poor old Uncle Edward who, after suffering further German food requisitions which cost him the last of his seed potatoes and all but two of our remaining chickens, was becoming increasingly worried about whether or not the Jerries would start commandeering the remaining milk cows in order to feed their troops.

The German *Feldkommandantur*-515, who would oversee the arrival of the Red Cross ship and be in charge of distributing the relief supplies, contacted my father in order to use the factory, with its already smoothly running set-up for the public ovens, as one of several storage centres where the civilian population could come and claim their individual food parcels.

The next day, on the Friday before Christmas, we all rode our bikes out to Grumpa's house at Archirondel, where we and other members of the family would spend the holidays together. Although I had seen my father load up the hay-box on his bike with a number of gift items destined to be shared over the holiday, I quietly wondered whether or not Father Christmas would be able to find the right chimney, seeing that my stocking would be hanging in another location when I woke up on Christmas morning.

On the following Saturday morning, Uncle Edward turned up on his bike, along with Old Maurice whom he had brought along to help with the slaughtering of Billy, the younger goat in the washhouse, Nanny having been spared for the sake of her precious milk. Straddling and firmly holding the goat between his legs, Old Maurice laid his hand on the goat's head, closed his eyes in a moment of silent prayer and then, before anyone could blink, he swiftly and expertly dispatched the animal with one quick sharp slice, allowing the blood to drain into an old enamel bowl. It was in sharp contrast to the slow, messy and painful method that had taken place in Nigel's garage.

Within a few hours, my grandfather, Uncle Edward, my grandmother and Old Maurice had all but completed the full butchering process between them. Permitting nothing to go to waste, I watched as Maurice took a hacksaw and cut the skull of the goat longitudinally in half, which allowed my grandmother to scoop out the brains with a large silver tablespoon. These were very practical, down to earth people with Edwardian manners and all the basic Victorian farming skills they had inherited. They had all been brought up with candle and gaslight, and knew how to live without all the modern era conveniences that many of my parent's generation had taken for granted.

When all the various spare cuts and portions of meat were wrapped and ready to be shared out amongst family and friends, Billy's hide was scraped, stretched and left on a frame to dry. Uncle Edward told Old Maurice to ride home with his and Old Marie's share of Christmas meat via the back lanes to avoid any chance of meeting some Jerries on the way, being accused of hoarding or black-marketeering and having the whole lot confiscated.

Despite all the miseries and difficulties that were being endured across the Island at the time, Christmas 1944 at Anneville Lodge may still be remembered as a joyful family event. Most of all I remember it as being warm. Grumpa and Maynard, the daily gardener who lived in a tenant house up the hill, had managed to quietly cut and collect enough firewood to keep a fire burning in both the drawing room and the dining room throughout the holidays. They had managed the task over a period without notice from German authority by gradually trimming the lower branches from some of the trees lining the *côtil*. Grumpa even provided us with a real Christmas tree that he set up in a corner of the drawing room. On Christmas Eve, we all gathered in the drawing room. After a moment of silent prayer for Uncle Bill, who was away fighting in the British forces, and for the war to end soon, Grumpa produced an old leather travel case containing a variety of pre-war Christmas decorations that grandma had carefully preserved from bygone days, and invited us to joyfully deck the tree.

Naturally, under Occupation conditions, Christmas 1944 probably turned out to be an extremely modest celebration for everyone on both sides of the divide when it came to the giving and receiving of gifts. Nevertheless, despite all of the wartime turmoil, Father Christmas did manage to get through and leave something for me under Grumpa's tree. Somehow, my father had managed to get hold of an un-punctured rubber bladder for my old football that we had had to stuff with straw. Now I had a ball that could really bounce, I couldn't wait to see the reaction from my friends and particularly from some of the older boys when I turned up to play with it in the bull field. However, the most enduring gift of all was to come from my grandfather. It was to be my first stamp album. He had partially filled the blank pages of one of his spare albums with a number of starting sets focusing upon British Empire issues in which he included a rare and valuable Edward VIII ten-penny misprint. For many years I would treasure and secretly develop the album into a respectful, and what today might be considered a prized, collection.

On Christmas day, the electricity supply came on from eleven o'clock in the morning for a period of about three and a half hours allowing those on the Island who were lucky enough to have electric cooking appliances to cook their family meal. For the rest of the population without any gas, it was either a wood stove – provided one had a log or two to burn – or the public ovens, and even they, including my father's ovens at the factory, were all struggling to keep going on the ever-shortening supply of fuel. Fortunately, at Anneville Lodge we had both an electric oven and a woodburning stove that allowed Grandma and my parents to roast the goat to perfection – blessing us with a most marvellous Christmas dinner and a family meal to be long remembered.

~ ~ ~

On Thursday, 28 December, we learnt, much to the relief of everyone throughout the Island, that the steam ship, SS *Vega*, a Swedish-registered Red Cross vessel, had arrived in Guernsey the day before. In addition, she was now due to dock in Jersey, where on the evening of the 30th German sailors would be waiting to unload her life-saving cargo of food parcels. For once, German efficiency played well to the benefit of the civilian population. Early on the following Sunday morning, New Year's Eve, transport, including lorries and horse-drawn carts, was lined up on the Albert Pier ready to be loaded with the Red Cross parcels, which was then delivered to the various pre-arranged distribution depots around the Island, the canning factory being one of them.

While we all attended the morning service at St Clement's Church and joined the rector in prayers of thanks for the international relief, my father rode to the factory to oversee the unloading and storage of the food parcels that would shortly be distributed to a very tired, worn out and hungry civilian population.

Except for listening to the Jerry troops heralding in their own cold New Year on an accordion in their billet across the road at Beauvoir, New Year's Eve passed quietly for my parents. Even though the curfew had been relaxed and extended until midnight they, like most others, simply went to bed early that night, thus avoiding wasting any more fuel on the fire than necessary. On this New Year's Eve, they could perhaps look forward to actually being able to open a Red Cross food parcel the next day.

"Oh Sax!" I heard my mother exclaim as they climbed the stairs in the dark together, "I do hope there'll be some real tea in the parcels. I'm just dying for a real cuppa – just so I can close my eyes, take a sip, and pretend for a moment that the war never happened!"

~ ~ ~

26 Salmon labels and salvation

January 1945 saw the weather turn bitterly cold. The soil in the garden froze and became like concrete. To make things worse, the electricity supply came to an abrupt end. Fuel for both heating and cooking became scarce and for some almost impossible to obtain. During the day, people from town took to desperately scouring the countryside for twigs and dried leaves and the odd branch from a tree – anything that could feed their stoves and fires without German apprehension. With no oil available for paraffin lamps, and candles fetching a premium price on the black market, I gathered with my parents around the dining room fire to open the first of our four allotted Red Cross parcels.

If there was ever an Occupation event that could be readily recalled, a remembrance shared by all those who survived the Occupation, then it would probably be safe to say that it was the moment when every family on the Island gathered to open their Red Cross parcels.

It was not necessarily some strategic wartime event destined for the annals of our Occupation history; it was more a personal moment, one that brought some light and hope into our lives; the very notion that somewhere in the world life was still going on normally, as it had done before the war. At least that is the way my family and I felt that night.

As a family, we had received a quota of four Red Cross parcels in all, two from New Zealand and two from Canada. Earlier in the day, while they were distributing the parcels at the factory, my father had found the name and address of a man in Montreal, together with a short greeting that he had written on the inside of one of the crates with the parcels. After the war, my father wrote to the man and thanked him and the Canadian Red Cross for their generous and much-needed help. The letter was later published in one of the Montreal newspapers.

My father decided to open the Canadian parcel first. My mother had already filled a kettle with water and had it ready simmering on the fire in hopes that the parcel might contain some real tea leaves.

The first item that was carefully lifted out of the parcel was a large can of

Klim (powdered milk), which I eventually learned to ingest by the spoonful when no one was looking. Then came a brown box with an American flag on its side, containing powdered eggs, which until my father explained the process, was something way beyond anything I could imagine. I mean, how do you turn a wet, sticky egg into powder?

Red Cross parcels arrive in Jersey, 30 December 1944

SS Vega unlaods in St Helier

Admiral Hüffmeier, Major General Heine and the Governor of Guernsey meet the Red Cross ship SS Vega in St Peter Port, Guernsey

There were several brightly labeled tins and cans containing butter, ham, Spam, bully beef, salmon and tuna.

"What's tuna?" I asked.

"It's a fish," answered my father. "Very nice. You'll like it."

"Really?" I thought to myself. "What about this?" I asked, picking up a brightly labelled can.

"That's real Canadian salmon," said my father.

I looked at the lovely coloured scene on the label. It showed a large fish jumping out of a river. In the background, green riverbanks led to a huge pine forest that climbed towards the snowcapped Rocky Mountains. For a moment my imagination drifted off into another world far away from our occupied Island to where I could see a Canadian Mounted Policeman in a red tunic riding out from behind one of the tall pine trees in the picture on the label.

Years later, while living in Canada and standing on the banks of the Kicking Horse River in south-eastern British Columbia, I would recall the dark days of the German Occupation when our lives were suddenly brightened by the vividly coloured picture of a jumping salmon on the side of a tin can.

"Here, let me have that," said my father pointing to the can of salmon in my hand.

Torn from the Mounted Policeman in my Rocky Mountain dream, I looked up at him.

"I can peel the label off for you without tearing it, if you like," he said. "And you can collect it as a … salmon label or for whatever you wish."

Much to my mother's delight, the parcels also contained packages of rice, flour, raisins, sugar, and coffee and yes – even some real tea, which she immediately set about brewing! An unexpected spark of enthusiasm in their conversation seemed to rekindle the tired embers of cheerfulness and warmth that had once existed between them on a daily basis before wearing themselves ragged with the struggles of the Occupation – it was something in them I had missed and all but forgotten.

They had met each other on the beach in 1935 and one day, according to my mother, while she was walking through St Helier with her own mother, they saw my father heading in the opposite direction across the street.

My mother spontaneously announced to my maternal grandmother, "That's the man I'm going to marry!" to which my maternal grandmother apparently replied, "Don't be such a ridiculous fool! You hardly know who he is!"

"Oh yes I do …" said my mother, much to the outright annoyance of her own mother, "I know exactly who he is and I'm going to marry him!"

"We should keep the old tea leaves," suggested my mother after satisfyingly draining her first cup of real tea in recent memory. "We may be able to squeeze another cup or two out of them before throwing them away."

"Yes, why not do that," said my father. "Best to make everything last as long as possible – just in case … never know what's coming down the road."

"Now, what on earth is this?" said my father, pulling a bright package out of the cardboard parcel and waving it in the flickering fire- and candlelight, causing its shadow to dance warmly across the dining room ceiling.

"Let me see … I wonder what could this be …" he continued, slowly and playfully spelling out the words on the package, "C-h-o-c … and this looks like another 'o' – and an 'l' … and an …?"

"Chocolate!" I exclaimed. "Is it real chocolate? Ooh! Let me see!"

And chocolate it was: a big, thick, chunky block of Canadian milk chocolate – for a moment it was as though the war had all but ended!

~   ~   ~

The first two weeks of January 1945 would turn out to be the coldest in living memory, with temperatures dipping to -6°C (21°F). Some of the Jerry soldiers, including Fritz, were still wearing thin summer uniforms under their greatcoats, and except for those who were on "combat ready" rations while engaged in special training and manoeuvres, signs of malnutrition were becoming clearly apparent throughout the overall German garrison. Despite the fact that the authorities were expecting the Red Cross ship to return within a month with 700 tons of flour on board, rumours began circulating that the Germans intended to announce a further cut in the general bread ration.

During this time, two American soldiers, prisoners of war captured and brought to Jersey after the fall of St Malo, managed to successfully escape to France in a small open boat. How they managed to accomplish this daring feat during a time of such cold weather was almost beyond imagination. Naturally the Jerries weren't too happy about the situation and began an investigation to find out who else might have been involved in helping them escape; fortunately nothing ever came of it.

Snow fell and settled to stay on the frozen ground. As we were still on our Christmas holidays, my mother bought some tickets for a matinee pantomime and local variety show performance held in a small community centre near the factory. My mother wrapped Diana in a thick blanket, put her in the small push-pram and we walked to the show. The snow was packed and squeaked under foot as we made our way along the pavement. Even though I wore my wellingtons with two pairs of socks inside, my feet – and everything else, became frozen stiff by the time we arrived.

The small theatre was packed with parents and children and although I'm unable to recall much of the performance, the memorable moment for me came when a pretty teenage girl included and sang a rude word – "bugger" –right in the middle of her song, which brought the house down in laughter!

After the show, we met my father at the factory where we were able to warm ourselves up in front of the big ovens while the last of the public came to pick up their hot evening meal before closing time. By the time we set out for home, it had begun to get dark and the temperature had dropped quite considerably. Within five minutes or so of setting off, my feet and hands were freezing. I already had a nasty chilblain on one of my little toes and it was so cold that I began to cry. When I slipped on some ice and fell, my father, who was also carrying a hay-box with our supper in it, had to stop and help me up.

"We'll be home soon, son," he said, taking one of my hands in his and holding it inside his overcoat pocket. "And we'll get a fire going so you can warm up in front of it."

My mother was also feeling the cold and became concerned about Diana – whether she was warm enough, even though she was bundled up in the thick blanket.

"Just imagine what some of those poor Russian workers are going through in this weather," she said. "Poor starving blighters with no heat."

After we arrived home, thawed ourselves out and had eaten our supper in front of the fire, I thought about what my mother had said about the Russians and how cold it must have been for them. I wondered how the poor worker with tarred feet and no shoes was faring on such a night, and why things had to be this way. My father tried to ease my concern by telling me that Russians were really tough and used to living in much colder weather than this.

"Don't worry," he said, "He'll survive this – whoever he is."

Of course, I realized that we had no way of ever knowing that.

"That's why they're giving the Jerries such a hard time on the Eastern Front," he explained. "'Jerry's' going to pay for all the pain he's caused when this lot is over – you'll see."

"When will that be?" I asked.

"Soon son," he said. "Soon."

~   ~   ~

27 Cold days and Nazi defiance

The awful bitter cold during the first two weeks of January 1945, combined with fuel shortages, saw a large gathering of half-frozen and desperately cold townspeople defiantly cut down a landmark evergreen oak tree on Victoria Avenue. At first, the Germans came storming in with armed troops under orders to arrest everyone and confiscate the wood for which they were ferociously fighting.

Fortunately, Baron von Aufsess appeared on the scene, and this sensitive man was so deeply moved by the sight of so many suffering people and the desperately defiant lengths they would go to in order to obtain fuel for their fires, that he immediately ordered the Jerry troops to stand down. Exercising his velvet glove approach rather than the hard-line approach preferred by Admiral Hüffmeier and the like, he allowed the people to continue gathering up what remained of the tree.

Ironically, on the next day, after citing military necessity, all the German garrisons across the Island began cutting down hundreds of trees to supply their own fuel needs. Von Aufsess' well-noted concerns about the harmful effects that unbridled deforestation might have upon the Island's natural ecology were not lost on my grandfather.

My father was also becoming very concerned about the fuel shortages, not just at home, but at the factory where they were struggling to keep the communal ovens going at the same time as being able to provide a minimal amount of steam for their basic operations. Despite the instant relief gained by one and all due to the Red Cross relief parcels, they were, in fact, a drop in the ocean when placed alongside some of the other problems everyone faced.

~   ~   ~

While the snow lasted on the ground, Nigel and I would wrap up as warmly as we could and join all the other kids climbing up and sliding down Callec's field on shovels, along with a homemade sled that had miraculously escaped being turned into firewood. When it got too cold to play outside we headed back to my place where we would warm ourselves up in front of the dining room fire and pass the time sorting out and swapping our latest hoard of salmon labels.

Children had turned to collecting and swapping the salmon and other labels that we found in our Red Cross parcels. There was a large variety of lovely coloured scenic labels to be had, all of them representing different makes and brands of tinned products. One of my favourites, besides the jumping Canadian salmon label, was the rare green and yellow label found on a tin of New Zealand butter – it was worth at least four of any other kind of label.

By the time the snow had melted and we returned to school, salmon labels – salvaged, scoured and collected from every dustbin and neighbourhood rubbish dump – had become so popular they almost totally replaced all the hard earned pre-war cigarette cards, military badges and souvenirs. Right up until the end of the war, salmon labels became the new school playground currency of choice, not to mention the source of many a lunchtime punch-up.

~   ~   ~

The Superior Council decided to hold back on issuing us with a second Red Cross parcel from the first relief shipment until they were certain that the *Vega* would return with resupplies, in particular a shipment of badly needed flour. Translated into schoolboy language, this meant no chocolate and no new salmon labels over which to fight or swap.

With no *Vega* in sight and no word of when the Red Cross vessel would be returning to the Islands, the German authorities cut the civilian bread ration in half. This came as a great shock. On top of this, to make matters worse the weather became very wet and stormy, thereby adding to the possibility of further delays. The foul weather also meant that the farmers, those who still had a few seed potatoes left in their barns, were unable to plough and prepare their soggy fields for spring planting.

Fortunately, on 6 February, amid the awful weather, the announcement came that the *Vega* had safely arrived and docked in Guernsey – but without any new shipment of flour on board! The next day, much to everyone's relief, the Superior Council issued everyone with a second Red Cross parcel (allotted from the first shipment) and our schoolyard business of swapping salmon labels got back into full swing.

After unloading in Guernsey, the *Vega* remained in port due to the continuing foul weather and was not able to steam for Jersey until the end of the following week. The main concern for everyone was the fact that the ship had left Lisbon without carrying any flour. Although this second relief shipment of Red Cross parcels did much to brighten our lives, the Island's overall resources were still at the point of complete exhaustion, causing an extreme state of tension between the occupying forces and the Superior Council over the basic needs of the civilian population.

~   ~   ~

By the end of the third week in February, the weather finally brightened to become pleasant enough so that I was able to ride to school without freezing my hands or getting soaked through with rain. I had been suffering with badly chapped lips and a nagging cough that was beginning to cause some concern on my mother's part more than on mine.

I met Titch and Drelaud at our usual place near the top of Don Road, from where we decided to ride towards the lower Grosvenor gate entrance to the College grounds and walk our bikes up to Prep rather than taking the other route up Mont Millais. On the way, we suddenly saw that nearly every house and wall had big swastikas and "V" for victory signs painted in black tar all over them. Naturally, the question of who could have done such a thing was on everyone's mind.

Eventually we learned that during the previous night a group of overzealous Nazi soldiers had tarred hundreds of houses and walls throughout the entire town. I remember feeling quite excited about the whole affair – even though it meant someone having to wake up and discover ugly, tarry swastikas had been painted all over the walls of their homes and properties. Uncle Edward's words quickly came to mind – he had told me that the Jerries already knew they had lost the war, but just did not want to admit it, as this tarry demonstration seemed to suggest.

The next problem was to decide how, when and by whom the tarry mess should be cleaned up. The people, who now found themselves with defaced properties on their hands, demanded that the Germans clean it up; naturally not wanting to admit to anything, the Germans flatly refused. Finally, the unenviable task fell to the Jerry Organisation Todt and their remaining slave workers, whom they had been unable to ship out before the fall of St Malo. The task would prove to be a far from easy one. As far as anyone knew, there was no kerosene on the Island that could be used as a solvent for the problem. All diesel oil and petrol held in reserve for military vehicles was unavailable. So the starving forced workers had to spend long hours hammering, chiselling and scraping the tar off the walls, leaving pitted scars that would remain and act as an ugly reminder for a number of years after the war.

~   ~   ~

Admiral Hüffmeier, 1945

At the end of February 1945, acting upon orders from Berlin, Admiral Hüffmeier, a devout Nazi hardliner, replaced Major General Rudolf Graf von Schmettow and took over as the new overall military commander of the Channel Islands. Many on both sides of the Occupation conflict saw this as a bad omen and were sorry to see the gentlemanly General von Schmettow leave the Islands on what could be a very dangerous flight across territory held by our own Allied forces.

Meanwhile, the Bailiff of Jersey, my grandfather and others on the Superior Council, who had long been aware of the growing ideological rift between General von Schmettow and Admiral Hüffmeier, knew that from then on they would be facing a very unpredictable hard-line Nazi who intended to see that every order from Berlin was obeyed.

Once in command, Admiral Hüffmeier showed little sign of any weakening of his resolve to stand and fight until the very end. Rumours quickly spread that Hüffmeier was already preparing for a series of small-scale spring raids on the Allied forces occupying the Cherbourg Peninsula. This was supported by the fact that a certain number of special troops who were actively engaged in preparations and local manoeuvres were being issued with extra rations, causing a growing display of open dissent within other branches of their army. The Germans were also starving, and a huge conflict started to arise between the Bailiff of Jersey and the German authorities over potato and milk supplies.

~   ~   ~

Worried about the state of my hacking cough, and afraid that I might be catching whooping cough, my mother decided to keep me home from school for a few days. Eventually, Dr Lewis came out to the house and listened to my chest with his cold stethoscope. His diagnosis was that I had neither pneumonia nor whooping cough, and, even if I did, with the chronic lack of medicine available on the Island there would be little they could do about it. But that being said, it might be wise to keep me home for a day or so.

By the end of the second day I managed to persuade my mother, by promising to wrap up and keep warm, to let me go outside and play for a while. So the next morning I got up and, after breakfast, headed for the tree house where I later met up with Nigel. He too, for some reason, had been let off school that day and had barely climbed up and settled into the tree house beside me when we both heard a massive explosion and saw a plume of smoke rising up on the skyline above the Palace Hotel, just north of College House where the Jerries had commandeered the hotel for use as a training school for officers.

From the safety of our little tree house we watched in fascination as the hotel was blown up by successive explosions, one after another, into smithereens and then burnt to the ground. At first, word had it that some disgruntled *Kriegsmarine* (naval) officer had placed a time bomb in the hotel where senior officers were expected to be attending a meeting. Some merit was given to this story by the fact that the Gestapo were known to be out searching for a member of the *Kriegsmarine* whom they suspected was hiding within the civilian population. It was also said, and it was more likely, that a small fire had been started somewhere accidentally in the hotel, and this had then spread to one of the ammunition stores.

A day or so later when I returned to school, Bob Sowden told me that the only thing I had missed about the explosion and fire was the loud clanging sound of a German helmet landing in the middle of the road just outside our classroom.

~   ~   ~

Uncle Edward had managed to collect a few logs together and light a roaring fire in the dining room at Hamptonne. It was one of those grey, damp and miserably overcast March days. One that was beleaguered and bound by wild blustery winds and light drizzle falling between the gusts – the kind of day we were taught to accept and endure each and every year in order to obtain some divinely elusive and extremely dicey guarantee for a hot sunny summer to come.

Grumpa and my dad were deeply engaged in a discussion about the explosion and fire up at the Palace Hotel when Elizabeth, her mother and her younger sister arrived to join the family for tea. Everyone had contributed something from their Red Cross package, including a teaspoon of loose tea leaves for the pot.

The *Vega* had recently arrived back in Jersey for a third time. Thankfully, this time she had arrived with a cargo of snow-white flour for the civilian population. Grandma had brought a batch of fresh scones that she had been able to make from her and Grumpa's ration of white flour. As kids, none of us knew what it was like to eat real white bread made from real white flour – the only thing we knew as bread was something coarse, brown and husky made from locally milled wheat. To top things off, Grandma produced a bar of Red Cross chocolate, which she gave to Elizabeth with the instruction to share it out between us kids. As for the adults, just being able to finally enjoy a real cup of tea together in front of a warm fire did much to cheer their spirits.

"Hüffmeier is all but impossible to deal with on any rational level," my grandfather declared angrily to my father and Uncle Edward "The swine now wants more milk for his troops – on top of which, he also wants the farmers to give up their meat rations!"

"What meat ration?" asked Uncle Edward. "They've taken most of our livestock – meat or milk, they can't have it both ways."

Old Marie, Uncle Edward's Breton housekeeper, brought in some more hot water to freshen the pot, and asked if Elizabeth and I would like to take a pot of hot tea out to the stables for Maurice and Charlie. This we were only too glad to do, thereby leaving the adults to discuss their wartime concerns and various matters of the day between themselves.

Scamp, the young wirehaired terrier, followed us excitedly out to the stables, peeing on anything that happened to take his fancy along the way. Charlie had just brought the cows in from the orchard and was busy bedding them down in their stalls when we arrived with their pot of tea and a small tray with a strainer and two enamelled mugs on it. Despite the damp, cold or blustery weather, the stables, bounded by what little hay and straw was left, always seemed to offer a certain air of warmth and cosiness.

"Ah, *wharro m'vier*," cried Old Maurice, who was delighted to see us, and quickly drew up a couple of milking stools.

"Ah, thank you my love ay," he said taking the tray from Elizabeth and placing it down on one of the stools. After which I handed him the steaming pot of tea.

"Ah *merci* m'boy you," he said.

Elizabeth and I stood back a little whilst he sat and, using the strainer, poured a mug for himself and one for Charlie. Old Marie had already mixed a drop of milk into the steaming pot.

"Hey, Charlie *m'vier*!" said Old Maurice turning to his brother, "*voici de thé* you."

Charlie dropped what he was doing, grabbed a stool for himself and plodded over to sit beside Maurice.

"Marie said to tell you that she put a full teaspoon of Red Cross sugar in there for you," said Elizabeth.

"Ah, that's nice," said Old Maurice lifting his mug. "Tell her thank you for me my love ay,"

Momentarily, Maurice squinted the wrinkled corners of his weathered eyes and looked at Elizabeth, before leaning to one side on his stool and cutting the loudest and longest fart one could have ever possibly imagined! I wanted to laugh out loud until Elizabeth quickly cut me off...

"Poo! Maurice!" exclaimed Elizabeth! "You rude stinker!"

"Ooh, me yes ay...!" said Maurice easing back onto his stool. "*Mais, le thé c'est bon m'vier.*

"Poo!" repeated Elizabeth, "You dirty sod!"

"Ah ... but thems what keeps my bum warm ay," explained Maurice. Besides my love you, them kind' a farts are better out than in, ay ..."

"Poo! Maurice, you're worse than a bloody German!" said Elizabeth, rebuking him.

"Ah, that one was nothing ay," said Maurice. "Only a number two bullet ay – ay Charlie?"

Charlie looked up from his mug of tea with a glazed look in his eyes to offer little more than a nod and a grunt of support for whatever it was that Maurice was talking about.

"You should'a heard my number one fart last week," said Old Maurice proudly, "The one I used me to blow up the Palace Hotel ay – ooh... a real number one Breton bomb fart him!"

Even Elizabeth had to laugh at that.

~   ~   ~

28   Tar on the wall before liberation

Shortly before we broke up for our Easter holidays, Admiral Hüffmeier did actually launch a series of small-scale raids on what was then Allied-occupied Normandy, beginning with an attack on the quiet little port of Granville. The successful raid caught the Allies completely off guard. And even though it did much to strengthen Hüffmeier's Nazi resolves to fight to the bloody end, it did little in the way of promoting any real fighting enthusiasm amongst the average malnourished Jerry conscript standing guard duty and left to wander through the country lanes gathering up stinging nettles in order to make soup.

Supplies of everything were now at a critical low. The only way to acquire anything was through barter. Every week my mother would search through the barter columns in the local newspaper: "Exchange lady's raffia sandals (worn once) for three eggs – Exchange lady's cycle for doe ferret – Exchange primus stove No. 5 for one hot water bottle – Exchange peas and bar of soap for sugar – Exchange half-grown rabbit for what?" Yet, while we were able to enjoy a limited ration of real white bread thanks to the SS *Vega* and her life saving cargo of flour, tensions continued to mount between the Bailiff, the Superior Council and the High Command under Hüffmeier.

Baron von Aufsess had been transferred and posted close to Hüffmeier's HQ in Guernsey, and any chance of the Bailiff or the Superior Council having a reasonable discussion or negotiation with the occupying forces quickly faded with the Baron's departure. Citing military necessity, the fanatical Admiral ordered the local farmers to deliver more milk and vegetables to his forces.

Across the Inner Road from our house, at Beauvoir, the Jerries who were billeted there, men who once marched in polished boots through the streets of St Helier, now spent most of their time trying to raise vegetables in the garden and guard their precious rabbits from being stolen at night. Their only consolation, albeit a hungry one at best, was that life in Jersey was still a whole lot better than being shipped off to fight and die on the Russian Front.

~   ~   ~

One morning, I woke to find that during the night someone had tarred the walls of Major Mourant's house from one end to the other – top to bottom with ugly black "Jerry bag" swastikas! At first I was quite shocked, and even felt a little hurt by the fact that someone would want to do what I thought was an unwarranted and spiteful thing to the Mourant family – even though the major may have been a grumpy old sod at times.

I was very fond of both Stella and Barbara, the major's two teenage daughters. I had been invited to tea at the Mourant's house on several occasions, and Mrs Mourant had given me Major Mourant's white regimental guard's dress belt and shoulder strap. Barbara, the younger of the two daughters, who was a little over sixteen at the time, was always very friendly, even going as far as to play stump cricket with me in the driveway. Every so often she babysat for my mother, looking after Diana.

I walked slowly along the lane towards the bottom of the long driveway where Fritz was standing guard duty, looking as I passed at ugly tarred swastikas and "Jerry bag" slogans scrawled across the walls of the major's house. Suddenly, through a half-open window across the lane from Fritz's post, came a ranting series of raving admonishments being expressed by a very angry Major Mourant, which broke the quietness of the damp still morning air.

"'Jerry bags!'" yelled the major. "In my house? Not on your bloody life – get up to your room!"

"But daddy!" cried Barbara.

"Now!" yelled the major firmly. "I'm going to thrash both your backsides – now get up there!"

The swish and whack of what I imagined to be the major's regimental swagger stick cutting across Barbara's bottom and then her sister's to the tune of their yelps, cries and sobs was enough to cause even Fritz to flinch in an animated expression of pain.

The uncomfortable question suddenly crossed my mind as to whether my mother might have been responsible – had she said anything to anyone about having seen the Mourant sisters flirting on the beach with a couple of Jerries the previous summer? She'd insisted we go down for a swim on the beach at Havre des Fontaines just west of Le Hocq Tower, rather than our usual beach at Green Island.

"Well, the tide's in," she had insisted, "and I'd like to swim somewhere different for a change."

Reluctantly, I'd agreed to go with her, and we took Diana along with us in her pram. The beach was quiet compared to Green Island (where most of my friends would be) and despite the fact that I found it a boring place to swim, there were some local people down there that day, and a load of German soldiers who were billeted just up the road, across from the fortified tower and slipway where Old Maurice would go to collect vraic.

My mother chose a soft sandy area on which to set the picnic blanket, she gave Diana a bucket and spade to play with in the sand, then lay back on the blanket to sunbathe with her eyes closed, while I ran down and took a dip in the water. When I returned and had towelled myself off, my mother, without opening her eyes, suggested I walk up the beach and say hello to the Mourant sisters who were sunbathing and chatting with a couple of men in black swimming trunks.

"I think the two young men they're flirting with are Jerry soldiers," said my mother. "If the major ever finds out, he'll skin those girls alive!"

True or not, the whole situation was beginning to make me feel very uncomfortable – if not angry. I just didn't believe Barbara and her sister were "Jerry bags" like some of the sluts running around town, and I didn't want to believe my mother could have instigated the unjust tarring and thrashing. But it has always troubled me. She may well have ...

~   ~   ~

My father would get up early every morning and go downstairs in his pyjamas and dressing gown to listen to the BBC News on his crystal set in the cloakroom. Ever since the visit and search by the Gestapo during the previous summer, I had pretty much guessed what he was up to. It wasn't too long before he began putting the earphones on my head and allowing me to hear the distant crackling of a BBC voice coming from London – not that I could understand too much of what was being reported, except for words like: advancing, Allies, troops, forces and German lines, which all sounded very positive to me.

"Won't be long – all over soon," he would cheerfully announce to everyone, including Mrs Elliot, before leaving for work. "They've got Jerry on the run."

On the other hand Admiral Hüffmeier, who was showing no sign of letting up in his determination to fight on until the last man, celebrated Hitler's birthday by coming over from Guernsey to Jersey, where he gave a rousing speech to his fanatical followers at the Forum Theatre. A few days later, Hüffmeier's hard-line attitude was seen to pervade when Nicolas Schmitz, a young German soldier who had fallen in love with a local girl, was dragged half-alive into the prison yard where he was shot as a deserter! Schmitz had hidden in his girlfriend's flat, and after capture he suffered terrible abuse at the hands of his Nazi guards before his untimely death.

Ironically, the following week we were happy to learn that Hitler had committed suicide in his bunker on Monday, 30 April.

Even then, early attempts at negotiating the surrender of the Islands to British forces was rejected outright by the fanatical Admiral Hüffmeier who, in utter arrogance, threatened to fire on any British vessel daring to approach within range of his heavy coastal guns.

By this time during the Occupation, the rest of the malnourished and ragged German garrison was all well aware of the fact that their war was lost. Being as hungry as they were, most couldn't wait for it to come to an end – if not for the sake of getting back to see what had become of their bombed-out country and families, but because as prisoners under the Allies they might have a better chance of getting something decent to eat.

German soldiers in the garden at Beauvoir
with their rabbits, 1944

In that interim, while German flags still flew at half-mast for Hitler, the Superior Council appealed for calm and order by asking people to avoid antagonizing the Germans, Admiral Hüffmeier in particular. Finally, on 8 May, in anticipation of the German surrender and knowing that British ships were well on their way to our waters, Alexander Coutanche, the Bailiff of Jersey, addressed an enthusiastic crowd in the Royal Square. Where at 3.00 p.m., when British flags would be allowed to be displayed once again across the Island, I stood with my father and grandfather to hear Winston Churchill's "Our Dear Channel Islands" speech over a public relay. There were tears in the eyes of many in the crowd that day.

Across the road from our house at Beauvoir, my mother, who had remained at home that day with Diana, told us that at about three o'clock, all of the Jerries billeted there ran out into the garden and hungrily killed all of their remaining rabbits and celebrated the end of their war with a hearty meal. The sound of their singing to a beautifully played accordion would last late into the night, and slowly everyone began to realize, that yes, the war was really over.

The next morning, during the early hours of 9 May, 1945, HMS *Bulldog* arrived off the coast of Guernsey. At 07:14 hrs, Major General Heine, accompanied by a young *Kriegsmarine* officer acting as Admiral Hüffmeier's envoy, stepped aboard the ship to present their credentials before surrendering.

Just after noon on the same day in Jersey, the Bailiff of Jersey boarded HMS *Beagle*, which was anchored out in the bay off St Helier, to witness Major General Wölfle and the Island *Kommandant* sign the documents and terms of surrender – our Islands were free and British again!

~   ~   ~

29   Celebrating freedom

Force 135, under the command of Brigadier Snow, landed and liberated the Island. Immediately, the "Tommy" soldiers, between handing out sweets and cigarettes to the hungry population celebrating the end of the war, began the task of disarming the Jerries and putting some of them to work cleaning up the Island, clearing mines and roll-bombs, and deactivating the abandoned military ordinances – a task that would last for many weeks. As for the rest of the German garrison, they were gradually shipped out to prisoner of war camps in England aboard the large US landing vessels that would sail in and beach on the sand in St Aubin's Bay.

One day, without daring to say anything to anybody, I decided I wanted to see if Fritz was still around. For some reason, for which I had absolutely no acceptable explanation, not even for Nigel or Elizabeth, much less for my parents, I wanted to say good-bye to Fritz. As soon as I got back from school one afternoon, I walked up the lane to the bottom of the long driveway leading to the house where Fritz was billeted. On the way I passed a couple of Jerry prisoners who had been put to work cleaning the black tar swastikas off the walls of Major Mourant's house. The Mourant family had been keeping very much to themselves and I had seen neither hide nor hair of them ever since the tarring incident. A couple of British Tommies were sitting idly on the low wall in the same place where I had first spoken with Fritz. They told me that they had been busy clearing the mines out of the back woods so that we would soon be able to play safely there again.

I was about to ask the Tommies if there were any Jerries still left in the houses up the long driveway when a large Bedford army lorry with a white star on its bonnet arrived and loaded both them and their Jerry prisoners into the back and then quickly drove off before I could broach the subject with them.

I walked up the driveway to the first house where I thought I might still be able to find Fritz, but the house was empty. Somebody had left the front door open, so thinking I might find a souvenir or two, I went inside and looked about. Abandoned household effects lay strewn about the place, but no uniforms, forage caps, helmets or badges. Other kids had probably got there first.

I reckoned that Fritz had obviously left and been shipped out along with his fellow prisoners of war and, sadly, I knew I would never see him again. Nevertheless, I also knew that I would never completely forget him.

Many years later, while working in Hollywood, I would recall and draw upon my fading memories of Fritz, fondly bringing them to mind as I sat and waited on the back lot of MGM studios, made up in full uniform as a Jerry soldier – boots, belt, bayonet and rifle, ready to go on camera.

The Germans leave.
May–July 1945

I was about to play my first two-line, guild-card, bit part in a show entitled *Combat*, a TV series starring Vic Morrow and Rick Jason. As we idly sat and waited for the crew to light the set, I thought about Fritz, recalling his little red German-English dictionary and the worn leather wallet in which he kept the picture of his wife and baby son. I wondered whether he'd been able to find and reunite with them amid the shattered ruins of his homeland. I recalled the way he slung and adjusted the rifle on his shoulder, the way he sometimes scuffed his boots on the gravel, the soft smile on his face when he reloaded his rifle after having just demonstrated to a group of little boys how it worked.

There were a couple of other actors on the set that day, along with the usual extras, all of whom were playing German soldiers, or so some of them thought. Only, I had seen the real thing, and for a few brief moments that day, after striding out onto the stage, "Fritz" suddenly appeared and played the Jerry part to the hilt.

~   ~   ~

It was on a Monday morning in early June when we arrived at school, not too long after all the excitement of the liberation, that Miss Cassimir promptly informed us that she would be teaching our class that day instead of Miss Painter. Miss Cassimir explained that over the past weekend Miss Painter and her family had learned the sad and shocking news from a French concentration camp survivor that her father and her brother Peter had both died in terrible conditions. Apparently, Peter had died of pneumonia in his father's arms during the previous November at Gross-Rosen, a notoriously brutal concentration camp in Lower Silesia, and that her father had frozen to death shortly afterwards in a railway box wagon on his way to Dora, an equally brutal camp located in the Hartz Mountains.

~   ~   ~

Supplies arrive from Britain
June 1945

Even though some of the basic necessities so desperately needed started to filter their way back into the Island, wartime shortages were still the order of the day. Ration books and clothing coupons were still required in order to purchase just about anything that might become available, and these restrictions would remain in place for many months to come. Many Islanders took to stripping the wood and insulation out of the German bunkers in order to feed their stoves and fires.

Of course, as kids in search of Jerry souvenirs, we spent most of our spare time scouring through the many abandoned Jerry bunkers, tunnels and various defence facilities. It became our favourite pastime, occupying every hour outside of school, offering a field day for all. Climbing over the big guns, playing soldiers and using the Flack 29 Oerlikon guns as a merry-go-round was pure unadulterated fun, and while the firing mechanisms in all the various defensive weapons had been removed, live munitions of every calibre lay scattered about everywhere in boxes and magazines. My best find was a case full of parachute flares, which turned out to be great fun to play with. We would gather at the rabbit patch in the front woods, where we would sit on the grass and extract the miniature silk parachutes that we found inside the casings. The little strips of magnesium that were also found inside the flare casings would in turn be fun to light with a match. We would then sit back and watch the dazzling brightness that they emitted when set alight.

One of the best places that we headed for was the large 4.7 Pak 35 Czech gun hidden inside the rotating octagonal hut up on Mount Ube, overlooking the quarry bordering the back woods. Except for the firing mechanism, which the Tommies had safely removed from the breach, everything else was in place, exactly as the Jerries had left it. Racks of live shells lined the walls behind the large gun, along with boxes of equipment used for maintaining the weapon.

It was not long before we were squabbling over whose turn it was to sit in the gunner's seat and drive the handles of the aiming mechanism to swing the gun into whatever direction and elevation took our fancy. I sat looking through the optical sight and managed to line up the crosshairs on College House, the former headquarters of the *Feldkommandant*, and offices of the German *Fieldkommandantur*-515. Drelaud took one of the heavy live shells down from the rack, carried it over to the gun and slid it into the breach. For a moment we all paused and looked at one another – the sudden thought being: "Even though the firing pin has been removed, this might not be such a good idea."

"We could hit the cap with a hammer or something!" suggested Drelaud.

"Don't be stupid!" cried Titch. "Are you crazy?"

"It could backfire and kill us all!" said Nigel in horror. Thankfully, everyone was in immediate agreement with him.

"You fool!" I said to Drelaud. "Take it out before we get killed!"

Drelaud pulled the shell out of the breach and looked about as if wondering what else he might do with it other than return it to the rack.

The Mont Ubé gun, hidden in a revolving hut above the quarry

Above: 4.7cm Pak 35 Czech gun – type used at Mont Ubé

Remains of the Mont Ubé gun today

"We could toss it over the cliff into the quarry!" suggested Maurice Etienne. "See if it goes off."

Drelaud turned and started to head for the top of the cliff overlooking the quarry below.

"Wait!" Bob Sowden yelled. "If it goes off it's going to make a hell of a bang."

"So?" questioned Drelaud.

"Well someone's going to hear it," I said, getting up from the gunner's seat. "And they'll come after us."

"Alright," said Drelaud. "I'll drop it over and then we can all do a bunk through the woods towards the bunker by Nicolle Tower – no one will find us there."

Without any further discussion, we followed Drelaud out to the edge of the cliff above the quarry from where we prepared to bunk off as soon as the shell exploded below – but nothing happened! All we heard was the loud echoing, clanking sound of the shell landing and bouncing across the granite rocks below – what a shame!

"Let's try another one," someone suggested – which we did! We tried dropping the next two shell casings first, hoping they might land on the firing cap and then explode – but they did not. Then we tried dropping the next batch of shells tip first, but all to no avail.

Surely, as is said, "God's mercy endureth forever," especially when He looks down and sees what little boys can get up to while no one else is looking.

I returned home that day with an optical gun sight in hand, probably one of the most expensive pieces of Jerry equipment that I had managed to get my hands on. My father asked me where I had found it.

"Near an empty bunker," I said.

"Well, it's very nice," he said looking over the scope. "But we'll have to turn it in because it's captured war material and as such, it belongs to the War Department.

"Damn it!" I thought to myself. "Better to wait before ever telling him about the Jerry bayonet hidden on top of my wardrobe!"

Needless to say in all of this, it wasn't very long before we heard all kinds of stories about kids blowing their fingers off while playing with live rifle ammunition.

"Mind you stay away from that stuff!" my father would regularly warn me each day during breakfast, lunch or supper, which meant about as much to me as "Don't be home late!" or "Do you hear what I say?"

~ ~ ~

30　Adjusting to freedom

Sometime shortly after the liberation of the Island, when most of the decommissioning was well in hand, a major military victory parade with a grand march-past and fly-past was held and widely attended.

Eager to see the parade, my father suggested that the best place to watch the event would be from high up near the entrance to Fort Regent. From there, we would be able to have an overview of everything that would be taking place below us. My mother decided to pack a picnic basket and make a day of it.

A couple of British Tommies now stood guard at the main entrance to the nineteenth-century fort, a far cry from a month or so previously, when the place was occupied and crawling with Germans. We secured a place near the wall across from the entrance to the fort, where many others with the same intent soon joined us to enjoy the wide sweeping overview of the whole area below.

From our high vantage point overlooking the harbour, we enjoyed a truly exciting day watching all the different branches of the liberating forces with their brass bands marching by in salute. It was a joy for us to see after suffering five long, lean years of jack-booted Jerries strutting around all over the place in their grey-green uniforms. It was certainly something for me, who as a nine-year-old child found it all very exciting – especially the fly-past of Spitfires, Hurricanes, Mosquito and Lancaster bombers led by three Gloster Meteor III jets, Britain's answer to the German Messerschmitt (ME-109) – oh, what a day!

While we were there, a mainland newspaper photographer came along and asked three passing British Tommies who were on duty up at the fort if he could take a picture of them in front of the entrance. They were of course more than happy to oblige. The photographer then asked if any of us would like to gather around the soldiers and be included in the picture, which of course everyone, including myself, wanted to do. The only problem as far as I was concerned was the fact that I was not wearing my shoes and I did not want to end up in a picture with bare feet!

"Don't be so damned silly, Geoffrey!" said my mother. "No one's going to see your feet – now get in there before it's too late!"

So at the last moment, just before the photographer clicked the shutter on his big newspaper camera, I reluctantly and somewhat embarrassingly ran into the frame, where I ended up standing slightly to the right of the smiling soldier whom I have always remembered since that day as the "Laughing Tommy".

A few months later, towards the end of our summer holidays, while aboard the cross-Channel ferry on our way to visit my maternal grandparents in England, we ran into the "Laughing Tommy", who remembered seeing us up at the fort. During a short conversation, he told my mother that he too was finally on his way home to see his family, after having been away for five long years fighting the war.

~   ~   ~

Commodities and basic household needs of all kinds were still rationed and very scarce. My mother managed to save enough clothing coupons with which to buy me a new grey flannel jacket and a pair of socks for school, which I proudly wore after what had seemed like a lifetime dressed in my old, worn out, homemade school blazer. Things were definitely getting excitingly better, but there were many changes to come, and in some cases disappointments were lurking in the air.

Elizabeth Colley left with her mother and sister to join her father in England, where after five years she'd finally be able to give him the big hug she'd so long dreamed of. The most disturbing thing of all for me was waking up one morning to find that Nigel and his family had also left the Island! The loss of my oldest and most trusted playmate was deeply disturbing for me. Nigel had simply vanished from my life, and this was something I had never expected – everything was supposed to get better when the war ended, not worse!

I was not the only one to experience such disappointments. One day at school, Drelaud told us that there was a store down in the central market selling oranges and bananas – wow! The most that we had ever seen of any such things were pictures in books or old pre-war magazines. Right after school we all hurried down to the market so that we might see the real thing for ourselves. Titch Cavey was particularly excited about the prospect and could not wait to get there.

Eventually, after dumping our bikes and running around the mostly empty market making frantic enquiries, someone directed us to a small store window on the north side facing Halkett Place, where we excitedly gathered with our noses pressed against the glass. There, right in front of us was what we took to be three huge oranges – they were gorgeous; the war was definitely over!

The fact that there weren't any bananas to accompany the oranges did not much matter too much; what we had before us was more than enough for four little boys to see.

Liberation, May 1945

Fort Regent

Yours truly standing barefoot right

"Oranges! See!" cried Drelaud. "I told you! Real oranges and you didn't believe me!"

"Wow! Look at them," I said. "Just like the ones Titch drew on his Christmas tree."

"Yes! But these ones are real," cried Bob Sowden. "I wonder what they taste like. I've never had a real orange – have you?"

I was about to answer when a passing woman stopped behind us and, looking over our shoulders, said, "Those aren't oranges! They're grapefruits! They're not oranges, oranges are different!"

Bitterly disappointed, Titch turned and looked up at the woman.

"They're not oranges?" he asked. "Not …?"

"No, silly," answered the woman before carrying on her way. "They're different. They're grapefruits!"

Titch looked at the grapefruit in the window for a moment before turning to Drelaud.

"They're not oranges," he said choking his bitter let-down. "You said they were … shit!"

As Titch looked back at the grapefruit, I saw a tear of pure devastating disappointment begin to run down his cheek.

"Well, they looked like … oranges," said Drelaud. "Geoffrey thought they were oranges too" he continued, trying to take the edge off things. "Didn't you?" he added looking at me.

"Come on Titch, let's go," I said putting an arm around his shoulder. "We'll get to see some real oranges soon – you'll see."

~   ~   ~

Just before breaking up for the summer holidays, and despite the awful loss of her father and brother, Miss Painter arranged a farewell party for all of us at her house up on New Zealand Avenue overlooking Victor Pallot's farm.

Drelaud and I had a great laugh over some biscuit cones that Miss Painter had filled with custard that wobbled rudely about, but after five years of near starvation, they tasted absolutely delicious.

Our next autumn term at Prep would begin in the original Prep school building at the bottom of College Hill where the Girls' College had been located and housed during the Occupation. Miss Painter would no longer be teaching us. Instead, we would have new teachers – mostly men who had been recently de-mobbed and returned home to civilian life – men who had served in the armed forces during the war.

Drelaud and I were the first to experience a caning from Hatton Thorne, the new Headmaster. He introduced us to the real meaning of pain, leaving bruising welts on our backsides that could last for a week! He even made a point of caning Bob Sowden on his birthday for some minor infraction of school rules, in order to celebrate the fact that both their birthdays happened to occur on the same day! Along with others, I generally regarded Thorne as being a bit of a sadistic bastard, and many of us began to miss the slow pace of the fun-filled days we had had at school when the Germans were still around.

Eventually, I suppose we all had to learn to come to terms with the new direction that life was unexpectedly taking for us after the Occupation, especially as it wasn't always exactly how we had once imagined it might be. I did my best to cope with the new school routine by focusing on sports and winning my colours.

Nevertheless, I did have my day when I stopped Thorne dead in his tracks. It was when Titch, in answer to some question during class said,

"We had more fun when the Germans were here – it was better then!"

"Don't be so silly!" said Thorne, his jaw dropping slightly in surprise. "How could you possibly say such a thing?"

"Yeah. It was better," came a murmuring mumble in agreement from someone near the back of the class.

"Yeah, it was," agreed several others in rebellious agreement.

"Yeah, I miss the old Jerries," chuckled Drelaud enjoying the dig at Thorne. "We had more fun when they were here."

"How?" demanded Thorne, clearly disturbed by what he was hearing. "How in God's name could your lives have been better – now the war's over?"

"Well," I said, knowing that I was about to slam headlong into some real painful trouble. "It was nice and quiet during the Occupation – before you and all the others came back and spoilt it for us!"

~   ~   ~

Mr Baverstock and his wife and daughter, who had been deported and interned in Germany in late 1942, returned to the Island, along with others including Peter Cardnell and his mother, to pick up their lives that had been so rudely interrupted. As materials and supplies from England started to filter back into the Island, Mr Baverstock reopened his grocery store on the Coast Road down at Green Island. My mother would phone in her weekly order according to whatever our ration books would allow, and Mr Baverstock would kindly deliver the groceries to the house, ensuring that we were the last delivery on his rounds, so that he might visit my parents and discuss their wartime experiences.

Geoffrey with mother, 1945

Geoffrey, 1945. Just after the war, wearing his new jacket and shoes

Graeme (Titch) Cavey on Liberation Day, 1945

1946 – the 880 yards. Far left: Michael Drelaud (the only picture found of him), far right: Geoffrey

Bob (Robert) Sowden, 1942/3

Nigel Meeks, 1940

My father managed to get his hands on the first post-war publication of a shockingly illustrated book entitled *Lest We Forget*, depicting all the horrors of the German concentration camps, in particular the camp at Bergen-Belsen.

At first my father thought it quite inappropriate for me to look at such a publication, but after some thought, he changed his mind and allowed me to look through it with him.

"Now you know what the Jerries were really up to," he said.

The pictures were unbelievably shocking and at first difficult for me to take in. However, when recalling the awful brutal beating given to the poor Czech worker just down the lane from our house, I soon began to realize that such unbelievable things could happen. In addition, even Germans such as Fritz would have to bear the awful stench and stain of this vile record upon their national character.

Mr Baverstock, or "Bavy" as my parents called him, took a moment to recall how on 19 November, 1944, while being held with his family at the Würzach Internment Camp, he had assisted with the arrival of some "exchange" Jews, sent from notorious Bergen-Belsen concentration camp.

"They were in a terrible state – all of them," said Bavy, slowly shaking his head. "I could never have imagined anything like it in all my life. The camp doctor came to me and said, 'Put on this white coat so you look like a doctor – I want you to see something.' I put on the coat and followed him into in the camp clinic and then on into his small office. I could not believe what I saw! There were two naked girls, couldn't have been more than teenagers, who looked like walking skeletons covered in greyish skin – it was absolutely awful – unbelievable! I hope they hang every last Jerry they can get their hands on – the whole bloody lot of them!"

I thought of all the Jerries who had been sunbathing in their swimming trunks down at the bathing pool and thinking that, when out of uniform, they all looked just like anyone else – just like us! They could be kind and decent like Fritz, or cultured like Baron von Aufsess. Yet how could they have done what they did? For many, this question remains unanswered.

~   ~   ~

31　Ghosts and strangers

By the time my mother, my sister Diana and I had returned from visiting my mother's parents in England at the end of September 1945, my father had hired a gardener to dig up the vegetable plots in the front garden and reseed them with grass in their place. Owners of gardens given over to wartime agriculture now began to replant them with flowers and shrubs instead of vegetables, and we finally had our own lawn to play on. Best of all, I got a new bike with real pump-up rubber tyres. The bicycle was one produced under the limits of a wartime economy. In short, this meant that it was all black without any hint of chrome on it. But riding to school became a whole new experience – not to mention the fact that the Island was now back to riding and driving on the left-hand side of the road, something we as kids of the Occupation had never known before. Gradually life, despite all of its post-war changes, was returning to some semblance of normality.

While some stark reminders of the Occupation remain evident to this day, others could unexpectedly rear their ugly head when least expected. A case in mind came for me one Saturday morning when I was playing field hockey on the front lawn with Titch Cavey, Drelaud and Peter Jones. Peter had just moved into Green Gates, the house across the road from Beauvoir, a house used and occupied by the Jerries during the war. As we dribbled the ball back and forth with our hockey sticks from one end of the lawn to the other, Drelaud looked up and, pointing down to the road at the foot of the garden, suddenly shouted.

"There's the kid who shot his brother!"

We stopped our play, and looking up I saw Freddie! He was hurriedly walking past us along the Inner Road on his way towards town. An awful numbness began to rise up inside of me, while the others began arguing over all the rumours and details they had heard concerning what had happened to Paul – Freddie's younger brother.

Apparently, one day during the previous autumn of 1944, Freddie and Paul had unexpectedly returned home to their cottage to find that a German officer had carelessly left his belt and holstered pistol on their kitchen table while their mother was busy entertaining him in her bedroom. Freddie took the pistol out of the holster and playfully began chasing Paul around the table and into their front room, where the pistol accidentally discharged – instantly killing Paul.

It was a horrible story and although I did not like Freddie too much, I suddenly found myself alone and apart from my friends and feeling absolutely wretched for him as I watched him disappear along the road.

Terrible incidents such as this could only have sprung up under the extraordinary conditions of a dreadful Occupation, nearing its end and ruled by dire necessity and want. Justice is only justice when it is tempered with mercy, and as Old Maurice would say, "there's more pleasure found you in forgiving ay, than in condemning by Chri."

The most infuriating thing of all for us was when a bunch of stiff-necked English officers came over and began clamouring for some sort of investigation into charges of collaboration with the enemy during the Occupation. A snobbish Major Stopford headed this slimy little squad of headline-seeking officials, with a Major Alan d'Egville and a Captain Dening supporting him. These men, in an arrogantly-worded memorandum based upon pure speculation and their ignorance of the true facts, had the cheek to refer indirectly not only to the Bailiff, my grandfather and other members of the Superior Wartime Council, but to all Jersey-men and -women, as being "Norman peasants of limited character and outlook!" This insipid martinet – who was not here, who had no idea what we had been through or how we had survived, pompously went on to question our loyalty, which he claimed we would willingly discard in order to protect our "parochial interests"!

At the end of the day, Stopford and his arrogant band of self-righteous cohorts failed to support a single case or charge of collaboration – completely exonerating the people of Jersey and their wartime leaders from any such suspicion.

~ ~ ~

The five years of Occupation and German totalitarianism brought out both the best and the worst in us, but it never broke the stubborn, ancient Norman spirit of the Jersey people. Instead, that would be broken under the post-war invasion and occupation by immigrants from the UK – people who no longer seemed to care for our old British values – "trippers" who came to the Island in droves, attracted by low taxes, cheap cigarettes and who saw it as an ideal place to avoid national service.

Eventually, the financial services industry would land upon our Island shores and thereby entice scores of speculative developers and outside construction companies to come and build upon whatever precious piece of soil they might grab. With a reckless disregard they would come and trample upon the very soul of the Island's traditional farming heritage, the *vraic*-rich natural pastures, even the cider apple orchard at Hamptonne would eventually succumb to the modern demands and an alien vision of social housing.

Men like my grandfather, Uncle Edward, my dear parents and others like Old Maurice with his exploding farts, knew our Island as a quiet place – an Island where, to paraphrase Ebenezer Le Page[22]:

> The climate was fair, the soil rich and well suited for growing vegetables, fruit and flowers, and a place God chose for breeding two kinds of creatures, Jerseymen and the Jersey cow.

For them, the Occupation would be the end of the Island, as they and the rest of our forefathers had known it. Times had surely changed. Except for a few fading remembrances, the Island would become a place of ghosts and strangers.

Like many other young Jerseymen, I would leave the shores of my Island home to live in faraway places, America and Hollywood to name but a few. And like many of my forefathers, I would return home to Jersey – where reminders of the Occupation remain to this day – the German bunkers with their concrete modifications and anti-tank sea walls still guarding our beaches.

A kid who was there during the Nazi Occupation wrote this book in loving memory of those he knew, and for all those who endured.

~   ~   ~

---

22 *'The Book of Ebenezer La Page' by G.B. Edwards.*

About the author

Geoffrey Norman was born in 1936 in Jersey in the British Channel Islands. After attending Victoria College he progressed to HMS *Conway* in North Wales where he trained for a career at sea. Following a tour of duty that took him around the world, Geoffrey emigrated to Canada in 1955, where he became a professional skier, teaching and competing in both North and South America.

In 1963 he moved to the United States where he subsequently spent most of his adult life. He founded Detroit's first pre-season, indoor ski school and, working with the *Detroit News*, introduced a skiing curriculum into the Detroit public school system. He then went on to create, produce and host *Ski World*, the first weekly televised live show devoted to the sport of downhill skiing to be aired in the US.

In 1965 Geoffrey moved to Hollywood where he worked as a camera operator and film editor on the NBC show, *Happy Wanderer*. Signed and represented as an actor by the William Morris Agency, he worked in a number of films and various TV shows that included Warner Bros' *Camelot*, *Rosemary's Baby*, and *Paint Your Wagon*. Geoffrey's film career spanned over three decades, both in front of and behind the camera where he enjoyed working primarily in post-production.

During the early 1980s, having sailed the international off-shore racing circuit along the southern California coast towards Mexico, sailing become his sport of choice. He skippered the racing yacht *Resolute* for many years. At the same time he pursued a passion for theology and eventually published the academically acclaimed commentary, *Meat In Due Season*. Later, aboard the

Resolute, Geoffrey penned the early chapters of *Philos,* a delightful allegorical tale of a wandering puli dog, based upon his true-life companion. A fully illustrated version is currently being prepared for publication.

The late 1980s found Geoffrey back in post-production at Paramount Pictures working on the *MacGyver* TV series, where he met Calvin Clements Jr. the show's supervising writer producer. Later the two teamed up and became writing partners, Calvin writing the Foreword to the present book.

After a short illness, Geofffrey Messervy-Norman sadly died in November, 2014 so that this memoir is published posthumously. He is survived by his partner Francesca Steele and by his loving sisters, Diana and Penny, in addition to many nieces, nephews, cousins and friends in Jersey and the United States.

Acknowledgements

The Publishers would like to acknowledge with thanks the permission to reproduce photographs and material supplied by:

The Channel Island Occupation Society and CIOS archivist Colin Isherwood
The *Société Jersiâise*
The *Jersey Evening Post*
The Jersey War Tunnels
The Blampied Family